Please return / renew by date shown.
You can renew ...   .uk
    or by tele...
Please have y...   ...dy.

D0513720

08 DEC 16,
16. FEB 17,   09. DEC ...
AUG. 17,
              24. MAR 22
10. OCT 17,
05 MAR 18,
30. OCT 18,
04 APR, 19,
27. JUN 18,
24. JUN 21,

Elisabeth Luard
Classic Spanish Recipes

Elisabeth Luard
Classic Spanish Recipes
75 *signature dishes*

hamlyn

An Hachette UK Company
www.hachette.co.uk

First published in Great Britain in 2012 by Hamlyn
a division of Octopus Publishing Group Ltd
Endeavour House, 189 Shaftesbury Avenue, London WC2H 8JY
www.octopusbooks.co.uk

ISBN 978-0-60062-348-9

A CIP catalogue record for this book is available from the British Library

Printed and bound in China

10 9 8 7 6 5 4 3 2 1

Both metric and imperial measurements are given for the recipes.
Use one set of measures only, not a mixture of both.

Ovens should be preheated to the specified temperature. If using a
fan-assisted oven, follow the manufacturer's instructions for adjusting
the time and temperature. Grills should also be preheated.

This book includes dishes made with nuts and nut derivatives. It is advisable
for those with known allergic reactions to nuts and nut derivatives and those
who may be potentially vulnerable to these allergies, such as pregnant and
nursing mothers, invalids, the elderly, babies and children, to avoid dishes
made with nuts and nut oils. It is also prudent to check the labels of
pre-prepared ingredients for the possible inclusion of nut derivatives.

The Department of Health advises that eggs should not be consumed raw.
This book contains some dishes made with raw or lightly cooked eggs. It is
prudent for more vulnerable people such as pregnant and nursing mothers,
invalids, the elderly, babies and young children to avoid uncooked or lightly
cooked dishes made with eggs.

Meat and poultry should be cooked thoroughly. To test if poultry is cooked,
pierce the flesh through the thickest part with a skewer or fork – the juices
should run clear, never pink or red.

Contents

Introduction

Behind the Spain of the tourist resorts and Mediterranean beaches, the elegant shopping streets of Madrid and Barcelona, the traveller will be aware of older traditions: hilltop villages shaded by olive trees first planted by the Romans; rice paddies watered by aqueducts set in place by the Moors; minarets as well as monasteries; and ports whose jetties were built by Phoenician sailors and that, in time, provided safe-harbour for treasure-ships laden with far more valuable cargo than gold – the botanical riches of the New World including potatoes, tomatoes, capsicums and all the storecupboard beans.

If history, geography and latitude dictate the daily dinner in Spain, the strength of traditional Spanish cooking lies in good raw materials simply and honestly prepared. Until recent times, safe behind the barrier of the Pyrenees and unaffected by what was happening in the rest of Europe, Spanish cooks preferred to concentrate on perfecting their own ingredients and culinary habits rather than take up anything fancy or foreign. Nevertheless, while recipes are fiercely regional – no Catalan would trust a Castilian to cook a *fideu*, and no Galician would trust a Valencian to prepare a *pote* – certain dishes are universal. Rich and poor eat alike, and the tortilla and the bean pot are the staples of the midday meal throughout the land.

The Spanish menu, as I learned when I was a schoolgirl in Madrid and later when I took my own young family to live and attend school in a remote valley in Andalusia, begins in the market place. By ten o'clock of a morning the inhabitants of Tarifa, my local market town, knew just what to expect of their daily rations. If the butcher had had a delivery of young beef from the Cádiz bull ranchers, that evening the town's earthenware *cazuelas* would fill the air with scented steam from a thousand tomato-rich stews. When the inshore fleet came in with a fine haul of silvery sardines or ivory-fleshed cuttlefish, or the migratory tuna shoals were running though the Straits on a spring tide, the breeze carried the fragrance of olive oil heating in a thousand frying pans. The Andaluz housewife has a reputation for skill with the raw-iron frying pan – she could, says the rest of Spain, fritter the sea spray if that was all there was.

Key ingredients

The quality of what's available in the market place allows the food to taste recognizably of itself. Meats are preferred sauced with their own juices, fish and shellfish are prized if they taste of the sea and vegetables are prepared as dishes in their own right and eaten in the proper season, as is fresh fruit for dessert. With this strong appreciation of quality comes a willingness to pay for excellence. Even the poorest will choose a little of the best if the occasion demands: a sliver of *pata negra* cut from the bone on the Whitsun pilgrimage to Our Lady of the Dew in the marshes of the river Guadalquivir, a few threads of real saffron to perfume the Sunday paella. Perhaps it's this, the certainty that comes from a long tradition of knowing how things should really taste, that allowed Ferran Adrià of the El Bulli restaurant, the most influential cook of our time, to change the way every chef now thinks and cooks.

Olive oil The defining ingredient of the Spanish kitchen is the pure raw juice of the olive. It's eaten with bread in much the same way as butter, used to dress vegetables and salads, in cakes and pastries and for frying, as well as stirred into the bean pot to thicken the juices. Home cooks rarely deep-fry, preferring to use a finger's depth of fresh oil to shallow-fry in a raw-iron pan. Spain's oil-production is traditionally geared to bulk, though this is changing as regional oils with a known and valued provenance have entered the market. The non-virgins are best for anything that involves the application of high heat, while cold-pressed extra-virgins are good for dressings, marinades and to enrich a cooking broth.

Jamón serrano Serrano ham, or mountain ham, is salt-cured and wind-dried without the application of heat or smoke, followed by a prolonged period of cellaring to develop the moulds that deliver the flavour. Most prized are the hams from the semi-wild ibérico, also known as *pata negra* (black foot) for its ebony trotters, which, when permitted to forage among the scrub oaks, earns the additional distinction *de bellota*, acorn fed. When judging excellence, flavour and texture matter more than tenderness. The best cuts are sliced off very finely from the bone (traditionally in short curls – *lonchas*) and eaten in the fingers with bread. The chewy little scraps are used to flavour soups, sauces and *croquetas*, or combined with eggs; the bone is sawn into short lengths and used in much the same way as a stock cube.

Chorizo The most obvious difference between the Spanish chorizo and Italy's salami, while both are all-meat sausages of similar preparation, is the inclusion of *pimentón*, or Spanish paprika, an ingredient that adds sweetness as well as colour. Salt is the main preservative along with (though not always) a light smoking. Additional flavourings include garlic, cumin, black pepper, oregano and red wine. If eaten fresh and soft, chorizos must be cooked; if allowed to mature – a natural process – the meat darkens and firms, and the casing grows a soft white bloom, when they can be sliced and eaten raw.

Garlic is the distinctive fragrance of the Mediterranean kitchen. Spanish garlic is mild and sweet, maturing on spring rain and early sunshine, and coming to Spanish markets fresh in the form of what looks like plump white onions. Nestling at the base of each layer are tiny pearl-like seeds, infant cloves that, when bunched and hung on a hook to mature, draw the juice from their coverings and swell. Once formed, the cloves are used raw as a rub for bread to eat with olive oil, or finely sliced as a dressing for marinated fish and salads (particularly tomato, beetroot and red peppers) or pounded to a mush with salt and olive oil to make an alioli; raw garlic is used in pickling marinades for everything from anchovies to olives. In cooking, their mildness and sweetness soften the flavour of anything cooked in olive oil; when high heat is applied, they caramelize deliciously. Spanish cooks pop whole heads of garlic into the bean pot and add handfuls of unpeeled cloves to anything roasted in the oven.

Spices and herbs Saffron, the stamens of an indigenous crocus, and pimentón, ground capsicums, are the home-grown spicings of the Spanish kitchen. Pimentón is available in mild, spicy or smoked varieties and is used in rice, stews and soups. Dried chillies, the poor man's pepper, and mild sweet peppers, *ñoras*, are used whole or ground to add flavour and colour to sauces, stews, rice dishes and preserved meats including pork dripping. Imported spices popular in cooking are peppercorns, cumin, nutmeg, cloves, coriander seeds, vanilla and cinnamon. Of the leaf herbs, flat leaf parsley is the universal favourite, with oregano, thyme and bay used both fresh and dried. Mint is partnered with broad beans in the Granada region, tarragon appears in salads in Seville and fresh leaf coriander replaces parsley on the borders of Portugal. Camomile, or manzanilla, is the most popular of the digestive infusions.

Olives To the Spanish way of thinking, olives are inseparable from bread and wine and should always be provided free in any bar. This suits the bartender, since a salt-pickled olive promotes thirst while lining the stomach with its oily juices – which, in theory, keeps the customer sober enough to carry on drinking. Spain's eating olives are gathered while still green and firm (or, if left a little longer, lightly tinged with purple) before they have a chance to ripen to black, the stage at which they are pressed for oil. In Andalusia, olives have long been a major export industry: the commercial olive canners of Seville export pitted and stuffed green olives all over the world; their canned black olives, however, are the result of deliberate oxidization rather than natural sun-ripening, so best avoided.

Sherry vinegar This is made with sherry wine that has been aged and matured by the solera method, and is mostly produced in the Spanish province of Cádiz. The flavour is stronger and more acidic than Italian balsamic vinegar, with a distinctive spiciness and a rich, oaky flavour. It's delicious used on salads but best used sparingly – dilute with its own volume of water when using to make a dressing or sharpen a mayonnaise.

Cheese The main protein source of the rural poor, cheese is prized in its own right and rarely used in cooking. In spring it's eaten as *queso fresco*, or fresh cheese, as a dessert with honey. The raw material can be goats', cows' or sheep's milk that, once renneted, is drained, pressed and comes to market as mature or semi-mature. Of the many regional variations, Manchego, the cheese of La Mancha, the central plateau, is deservedly most famous. Dairy country – Asturias and the land of the Basques – produces a pair of distinguished blue-veins, Cabrales and Idiazabal.

Almonds The Moors, the colonial power in Andalusia for seven centuries, planted their borrowed hillside with stock from the Jordan Valley. As a result, almonds, both ground and whole, are used a great deal in the Spanish kitchen. They are used to thicken sauces and in nut milk preparations, such as Granada's *ajo blanco* (see page 36), and in the making of nougats, marzipans and two Christmas sweetmeats – *polverones* (see page 147), powdery cinnamon-flavoured cookies shortened with lard, and the halva-like *turron*.

Bread Country loaves, or *pan candela* – round or oval for portability, raised with leaven from the day before and baked in a wood-fired oven (although rarely these days) – are rough-textured, chewy and robust, with an elastic, creamy-white crumb and a thick golden-brown crust. They are sold by weight rather than volume. It dries to palatable crusts which are used for stale bread dishes – *migas* and other soaked-bread preparations including the original gazpacho, a thick bread porridge eaten hot in winter and cold in summer. The most popular town bread is the torpedo-shaped *bolillo*, a bread roll with a snowy, dense-textured crumb and a thick, soft brown crust. Breakfast breads include the Mallorcan *saimaza*, snail-shaped buns enriched with lard and sweetened with dried fruits, and *churros*, tubular doughnuts made with naturally leavened batter fried to order in street kiosks and eaten with steaming cups of coffee or hot chocolate.

Lard *Manteca*, pure pork lard, is used in baking and to enrich stews and sauces instead of butter. It comes in three forms: pure white and plain for pastry and cookies; *manteca colorada*, lightly salted lard coloured red with pimentón (Spanish paprika), flavoured with garlic and used as a spread on bread or for stirring into the bean pot; and *manteca colorada con carne*, flavoured lard in which small pieces of pork or chorizo are preserved.

Tapas

Mushrooms with Garlic and Parsley
Setas a la parilla

SERVES 4

500 g (1 lb) fresh large, open-capped wild or cultivated mushrooms

1 tablespoon olive oil

2 garlic cloves, finely chopped

1 tablespoon dried oregano

2 tablespoons finely chopped parsley

salt and freshly milled black pepper

toasted sourdough bread, to serve

The Basques and Catalans are the mushroom fanciers of Spain. An astonishing variety of wild fungi are gathered, the most popular being the saffron milk cap – a meaty mushroom found in pine woods that produces a milky juice and has an alarming habit of bruising blue.

1 Shake the mushrooms to evacuate any unwelcome residents and wipe the caps – don't rinse or peel. Trim off the stalks close to the base.

2 Trickle the mushrooms with the oil and salt lightly. Place them on a preheated griddle or barbecue, cap-side to the heat, and grill fiercely until the juices pool in the gills. If you want to use an overhead grill, you will have to cook the undersides of the mushrooms first.

3 Sprinkle the gills with the garlic, oregano and parsley, season with plenty of pepper and cook for another couple of minutes. Serve on thick slabs of toasted sourdough bread to catch the juices.

Toasted Almonds
Almendras tostadas

SERVES 8−10

500 g (1 lb) whole unblanched almonds

1 tablespoon olive oil

1 teaspoon salt

1 free-range egg white, beaten with its own volume of water

1 tablespoon pimentón (Spanish paprika)

1 teaspoon ground coriander

1 teaspoon ground cumin

Although these are available commercially, almonds warm from the oven are irresistible. Prepare them fresh.

1 Scald the almonds with boiling water and pop them out of their skins as soon as the water is cool enough for your fingers – my children loved the task as much as they appreciated the result.

2 Brush a baking tray with the oil. Spread the skinned almonds out in the oiled baking tray, shake to coat the nuts with the oil and sprinkle with the salt. Place in a preheated oven, 180°C (350°F), Gas Mark 4, for 15–20 minutes, or until just golden – shake regularly to avoid sticking and don't let them brown. A perfectly toasted almond squeaks when you bite it. Alternatively, place in a cooler preheated oven, 150°C (300°F), Gas Mark 2, and double the roasting time – temperature is not as important as a watchful eye.

3 Allow to cool to finger-hot, then toss with the egg white mixture – a precaution that allows the spices to stick to the almonds. Sprinkle with the spices, shake to coat and return to the oven for a moment to set the coating. Leave to cool before storing in an airtight tin.

Green Olives with Herbs and Spices

Aceitunas aromatisadas

SERVES 8-10

about 1 litre (1¾ pints) water

500 g (1 lb) plain-brined green olives

3–4 garlic cloves, unpeeled and roughly chopped

1 teaspoon crumbled dried thyme

1 teaspoon aniseed or fennel seeds

1 Seville orange or lemon

3–4 tablespoons sherry or white wine vinegar

This is an easy method of giving commercially prepared green olives a home-pickled flavour, particularly if made with the big green olives of Seville. Choose Spanish olives for this dish such as manzanillas, gordal or reina, if you can.

1 Boil the water and then leave it to cool.

2 Drain the olives and mix them with the garlic, thyme and aniseed or fennel seeds.

3 Cut a thick slice from the middle of the orange or lemon and set it aside, then chop the rest of the fruit, skin and all. Add the chopped fruit to the olives and pack everything in a well-scrubbed and scalded jar. Pour in the sherry or vinegar and enough of the cooled water to cover, then top with the reserved slice of fruit, pushing it down to keep the olives submerged.

4 Seal tightly and leave in the refrigerator for at least a week to take the flavours. The olives keep well, refrigerated, for 3–4 weeks.

Chilli-roasted Chickpeas
Garbanzos tostados picantes

SERVES 8

500 g (1 lb) dried chickpeas, soaked overnight in cold water

olive oil, for oiling

1 teaspoon chilli flakes

sea salt

My children loved these crisp, nutty little nibbles, although I had to go easy on the chilli. Sold hot from the roasting pan at féria *time (the annual summer festival) in the villages of Andalusia, they are the poor man's salted almond.*

1 Drain the chickpeas thoroughly and dry them in a clean cloth or with kitchen paper.

2 Spread them in a single layer on a lightly oiled baking tray. Place in a preheated oven, 150°C (300°F), Gas Mark 2, for about an hour until dry, crisp and golden. Shake regularly to avoid sticking. Alternatively, dry-fry the drained chickpeas over the lowest possible heat – be careful, as they jump like popcorn.

3 Toss with the chilli flakes and a little sea salt. To store, leave to cool (don't salt or add chilli) and pack in a jar with a well-fitting lid.

Chilli Potatoes
Patatas bravas

SERVES 4

small bottle olive oil, about 200 ml (7 fl oz)

12 dried chillies

1 kg (2 lb) floury potatoes, peeled and cut into fat fingers or cubes

oil, for frying

salt

There are many versions of this recipe, but here's how they make them at the Bar Tomás in Barcelona, where everyone who's anyone goes for their midday treat. Allow at least a week for the chilli to impart its fire and colour to the oil.

1 Pour most of the olive oil from the bottle into a jug. Pack the chillies into the bottle and top up with as much of the olive oil as will fit. Seal tightly and leave for a week before using.

2 Salt the potatoes and leave them to drain in a sieve for about 10 minutes. Shake to remove excess moisture, but don't rinse.

3 Heat the oil for frying in a deep frying pan until a faint blue haze rises. Slip in the potatoes and fry gently, a batch at a time, until soft. Remove and drain. Reheat the oil and fry them again until crisp and golden. Repeat if necessary – which, depending on the choice of potato, it may well be.

4 Dress the potatoes with the chilli-infused olive oil – or hand round separately, for dipping. You can hand round a garlicky mayonnaise as well, just for good measure.

Meatballs in Tomato Sauce
Albondigas en salsa

SERVES 4

SAUCE

500 g (1 lb) ripe fresh or canned tomatoes

2 tablespoons olive oil

1 onion, finely chopped

1 garlic clove, finely chopped

1 red pepper, cored, deseeded and finely chopped

1 small glass dry sherry or red wine

1 small cinnamon stick

1 bay leaf

salt

MEATBALLS

350 g (11½ oz) minced meat (pork and beef)

1 free-range egg, beaten

100 g (3½ oz) fresh breadcrumbs

1 garlic clove, very finely chopped

1 onion, very finely chopped

1 tablespoon chopped parsley

1 teaspoon ground cumin

1 teaspoon ground coriander

salt and freshly milled black pepper

seasoned plain flour, for dusting

2–3 tablespoons olive oil, for frying

Tasty meatballs are the frugal Spanish housewife's standby. Cheap and easy to divide into small portions, they're the perfect tapa. The proportion of breadcrumbs to meat can be varied to suit your purse.

1 Attend to the sauce first. If using fresh tomatoes, scald, skin and chop the flesh. In a small saucepan, heat the oil and fry the onion and garlic until they soften and take a little colour. Add the tomatoes, red pepper, sherry or wine and the cinnamon stick. Add the bay leaf and season with salt. Bubble up for a moment, then turn down the heat and leave the sauce to simmer and reduce while you make the meatballs.

2 Work all the meatball ingredients together thoroughly – the more you work it, the better. With wet hands (keep a bowl of warm water handy for dipping your fingers), form the mixture into little bite-sized balls. Dust them through a plateful of seasoned flour.

3 Heat the oil for frying in a deep roomy frying pan, slip in the meatballs and fry, turning carefully, until firm and lightly browned on all sides. Add the tomato sauce, bubble up and simmer gently for about 20 minutes until the meatballs are tender. Serve with crisp lettuce leaves for scooping or, for a more substantial meal, chunks of crusty country bread or plain white rice.

Chicken Croquettes
Croquetas de pollo

SERVES 6

4 tablespoons olive oil

125 g (4 oz) plain flour

600 ml (1 pint) hot
  chicken stock (from
  the puchero pot, or
  freshly made)

1 teaspoon ground
  allspice

½ teaspoon freshly
  grated nutmeg

seasoned plain flour, for
  dusting

1–2 free-range eggs,
  lightly beaten with a
  little water

plateful of fresh
  breadcrumbs

oil, for frying

salt and freshly milled
  black pepper

Croquetas require dexterity and patience, but a crisp coating and a melting, creamy interior reward the effort. The basis is a thick panada made with a well-flavoured broth, which may or may not be combined with additional flavourings: diced serrano ham, crabmeat, chopped prawns or grated cheese.

1 Heat the olive oil in a small saucepan and stir in the flour. Lower the heat and stir for a moment or two until it looks sandy (don't let it brown). Whisk in the hot stock in a steady stream until you have a smooth, thick sauce. Season with salt and pepper, the allspice and nutmeg. Beat the sauce over a gentle heat for 10 minutes to cook the flour. Spread in a dish, then leave to cool, cover with clingfilm and set in the refrigerator to firm – overnight is best.

2 With wet hands (keep a bowl of warm water handy for dipping your fingers), form the mixture into little bite-sized bolsters. Dust them through the flour, coat with the egg mixture and then press into the breadcrumbs to make a perfect jacket. Refrigerate for at least another hour – overnight, if possible – to set the coating. You can, if you wish, freeze a batch ready for later.

3 When you're ready to serve, heat enough oil to submerge the *croquetas* completely until a faint blue haze rises. Slip in the *croquetas* straight from the refrigerator, a few at a time to avoid lowering the temperature of the oil. If the coating splits open, the oil is too hot; if it doesn't crisp and seal within a minute, it's too cool. Remove the *croquetas* with a slotted spoon as soon as they're crisp and brown, and transfer to kitchen paper. Serve without delay, while they're still piping hot.

Moorish Kebabs
Pinchitos moruños

SERVES 6–8

500 g (1 lb) lamb or
pork, trimmed and
diced into small
pieces

2 tablespoons olive oil

1 teaspoon ground
cumin

1 teaspoon ground
coriander

1 teaspoon pimentón
(Spanish paprika)

1 teaspoon turmeric

½ teaspoon salt

½ teaspoon freshly
milled black pepper

baguette or ciabatta
bread, cubed, to serve

Long skewers threaded with scraps of spiced meat rarely appear on restaurant menus unless aimed at tourists, but they are a speciality of féria *time (summer fiesta), cooked to order on a little charcoal brazier by an itinerant peddler resplendent in a scarlet fez.*

1 Check over the meat – all the pieces should be neatly trimmed and no bigger than a baby's mouthful.

2 Combine the oil with the flavourings and turn the mixture thoroughly with the meat. Cover and leave in a cool place overnight to take the flavours.

3 Thread the meat on to 8 bamboo or fine metal skewers – about 6–7 little pieces each. If using bamboo skewers, soak them in water for 30 minutes first.

4 Cook the meat under a preheated grill or on a preheated barbecue over a high heat, turning the skewers frequently, until well browned but still juicy. Serve on the skewers, with a cube of bread speared on the end of each so that people can pull the meat off without burning their fingers.

Grilled Sardines
Sardinas a la parilla

1 kg (2 lb) whole fresh sardines

sea salt

This is the most popular way of preparing the fat sardines trawled by the inshore fleets. Fresh-caught sardines flash a brilliant rainbow of colour, their eyes bright and shiny. Don't scale them − the scales and the natural oil in the skin stop them sticking to the grate.

1 Gut the sardines, leaving their heads and tails in place − easily done with your forefinger through the soft bellies − and rinse to remove the loose scales. Salt generously.

2 Place the fish under a preheated grill or on a preheated griddle (Spanish cooks use a steel plate heated from beneath) and grill fiercely, turning once, until the skin blisters black and bubbly. The thicker the fish, the longer they will need, but 3−4 minutes on each side should be ample.

3 Serve one fish per tapa, with a lemon quarter. To eat, pick up the fish by the tail, holding the head with the fingers and thumb of the other hand, and eat straight down the bone, removing the fillets with your teeth. No one with any sense eats a grilled sardine with a knife and fork. You'll need chunks of bread for wiping fishy fingers.

Roast Red Peppers with Anchovies

Pimientos asados con anchoas

SERVES 4

4 red peppers

2 tablespoons extra-virgin olive oil

50 g (2 oz) can salt-pickled anchovies in oil, drained

black pepper

The sweet flesh of the peppers perfectly complements the salty fillets of anchovy – the best are packed straight from the cold waters of the Bay of Biscay in the canneries of Asturias and Galicia. Choose ripe red bell peppers or the scarlet triangular peppers from sunny Rioja.

1 Roast the peppers whole by holding them over a gas or candle flame, speared on the end of a knife, until the skin blisters and blackens. Alternatively, place them in a preheated oven, 240°C (475°F), Gas Mark 9, for 15–20 minutes, turning them halfway through.

2 Seal the peppers in a plastic food bag, wait for 10 minutes for the skin to loosen, then peel with your fingers. Deseed and cut the flesh into triangles or ribbons, depending on the original shape of the pepper.

3 Place the peppers in a single layer on a plate and trickle with the olive oil. Arrange the anchovies decoratively over the top and finish with a grinding of black pepper. Serve accompanied with plenty of crusty bread to mop up all the delicious juices.

Prawns with Garlic and Chilli
Gambas pilpil

SERVES 4
350 g (11½ oz) raw
  peeled prawns
4 tablespoons olive oil
1 garlic clove, sliced
1 teaspoon small dried
  chillies, deseeded
sea salt

Tapa bars that specialize in these mouth-scalding preparations provide customers with little wooden forks so that they don't burn their lips. Angulas, *or baby eels, are prepared in the same way, as are hake throats,* kokochas, *a speciality of the Basque Country.*

1 Pick over the prawns and remove any stray whiskers.

2 The important thing about this simple dish is that the prawns must be sizzling hot when they are served, ideally in the dish in which they are cooked. With this in mind, choose small individual earthenware casseroles (*cazuelas*) that have been tempered to withstand direct heat (see page 41). Alternatively, use a frying pan to cook the prawns, and heat individual ramekin dishes in the oven for serving.

3 Heat the oil until a faint blue haze rises and add the garlic and chillies. Reheat until sizzling, then add the prawns and let them cook. They'll turn opaque almost immediately. Serve as soon as the oil spits and bubbles in their individual casseroles or heated ramekins, with chunky bread for mopping up the fiery oil. Hand the sea salt round separately.

Clams in Sherry
Almejas en vino de Jerez

SERVES 4−6

2 tablespoons olive oil

2 garlic cloves, finely chopped

1 kg (2 lb) live bivalves, such as clams, cockles, mussels or razor shells, cleaned (see page 99)

1 large glass dry sherry or white wine

2 tablespoons chopped parsley

a little sugar

salt and freshly milled black pepper

Bivalves have a relatively long shell life, surviving for as long as they can keep water in their shells — hence the need to reject those with cracked shells or that remain closed when cooked. Spanish housewives expect to buy them live in the shell, the only guarantee of freshness.

1 Heat the oil in a saucepan, add the garlic and let it soften for a moment. Tip in the shellfish, then add the sherry or wine and the parsley. Season with salt and pepper and the sugar, and turn up the heat. As soon as steam rises, cover with a lid and leave to cook, shaking the pan to redistribute the shells. Allow 3−4 minutes for all the shells to open — check and turn them over if necessary. Discard any shells that remain closed.

2 Remove the pan from the heat as soon as the shells are open and serve straight from the pot — never mind if they cool down to room temperature, which happens very swiftly. Don't reheat or they'll be rubbery. Leftovers can be served with a little dressing of chopped tomato, parsley and onion.

3 Serve in deep plates and eat with your fingers, providing plenty of country bread for mopping up the juices.

Frittered Squid

Calamares a la romana

SERVES 4-6

500 g (1 lb) cleaned
  squid or cuttlefish,
  sliced into rings,
  tentacles left whole
  (see page 94)

about 4 tablespoons
  strong bread flour

1 tablespoon semolina

oil, for deep-frying (a
  mixture of olive and
  sunflower is good)

sea salt

quartered lemons, to
  serve

Squid (calamares) *and cuttlefish* (chocos) *are both suitable for the treatment – simply flipping the prepared fish through flour to give it a light coating that crisps in the fryer. Small specimens (no bigger than a teaspoon) can be fried whole, just as they come from the sea.*

1 Rinse, drain and shake the fish to remove excess moisture (don't dry it completely).

2 Spread the flour mixed with the semolina on a plate (no salt). Working quickly, dust the fish through the flour a few pieces at a time – the surface should be damp enough for the flour to form a coating – then drop into a sieve and shake to remove the excess flour.

3 Meanwhile, heat the oil in a deep-fryer or heavy frying pan. Test the temperature of the oil with a bread cube: it's ready for frying when bubbles form around the edge immediately and the crumb turns golden within a few seconds. Drop the coated fish into the hot oil quickly in batches and fry until golden and crisp, turning once. Transfer to kitchen paper to drain.

4 Serve piping hot and without reheating (reheating makes cephalopods rubbery), lightly salted and accompanied by lemon quarters.

Chilled Tomato and Garlic Soup
Gazpacho

SERVES 4

2 slices of day-old
  bread (about 50 g/2 oz)
ice-cold spring water,
  for soaking and
  thinning
2 tablespoons wine
  vinegar
2 garlic cloves, crushed
2 tablespoons olive oil
1 small or ½ large
  cucumber, peeled and
  roughly chopped
1 kg (2 lb) ripe tomatoes,
  skinned, deseeded
  and chopped
1 green pepper, cored,
  deseeded and roughly
  chopped
a little sugar
salt

In its modern form, this is a refreshing chilled tomato soup. In Spain, it's a way of making last week's bread palatable by soaking it with fresh water and flavouring it with a sprinkle of vinegar, garlic and oil. Here's the modern version; embellish it as you please.

1 Put the bread to soak in a few tablespoons of ice-cold spring water with the vinegar and garlic. Drop into a liquidizer or food processor and process to a purée, or pound in a mortar with a pestle. Add the oil and remaining vegetables. Add ice-cold spring water until you have the consistency you like – thick or thin, depending on whether you mean to serve it as a refreshment or a soup.

2 Adjust the seasoning with salt and the sugar. Transfer to a jug and cover securely. Set in a cool place or the refrigerator for 2–3 hours, or until well chilled. No ice – it just dilutes the delicate flavour and replaces it with the taste of the refrigerator instead.

3 As a refreshment, serve in a chilled glass, with a little olive oil drizzled on top. As a first-course soup, ladle into bowls and hand round any extras separately. Choose from diced bread croutons fried in a little olive oil (only worth it if you make your own), chopped hard-boiled egg, diced serrano ham, cucumber, peppers, tomato or mild Spanish onion.

White Gazpacho
Ajo blanco

SERVES 6-8

1 slice of yesterday's
bread, crusts removed

100 g (3½ oz) whole
blanched almonds

2 garlic cloves, peeled

1 tablespoon olive oil

1 tablespoon white wine
vinegar

1 litre (1¾ pints) cold
water

sugar, to taste

salt

a few small white
grapes, peeled and
deseeded, to serve

*A sophisticated summer refresher from Granada, white gazpacho is
made with an infusion of almond milk heavily perfumed with garlic.
You don't need much of it – it has a kick like a mule. I like to serve
it in a little tumbler with another of red gazpacho and a glass of
chilled dry sherry.*

1 Put the bread, almonds, garlic, oil, vinegar and 500 ml
(17 fl oz) of the water into a liquidizer or food processor
and process thoroughly. Add enough water – another
500 ml (17 fl oz) or so – to give the consistency of thin
milk. Season with sugar and salt to taste. Transfer to a jug,
cover, and chill thoroughly.

2 To serve, pour into small bowls or glasses and try to
float a couple of grapes on top of each serving. Mine
always drop to the bottom. No matter – it'll make a nice
surprise at the end. Warn participants that this is a high-
garlic area.

Garlic Soup
Sopa de ajo

SERVES 4

6 tablespoons olive oil

6 thick slices of robust country bread, cut into cubes

12 fine fat garlic cloves, crushed

1 tablespoon pimentón (Spanish paprika)

about 1 litre (1¾ pints) chicken stock or water

4 free-range eggs

salt and freshly milled black pepper

More than a flavouring, garlic is a philosophy, a declaration of otherness, a way of life. Here, in a simple soup that is given to invalids and babies as well as their elderly relatives, it's cooked to a gentle sweetness that soothes the spirit and calms the stomach.

1 Warm the oil in a heavy pan, and as soon as it's hot enough to fry, drop in the bread cubes and the garlic. Fry gently and patiently until the garlic softens and the bread is golden – don't let it brown. Stir in the pimentón and add the stock or water. Season lightly with salt and pepper, then bring to the boil, cover and cook for 5 minutes, or until the bread is spongy and has soaked up most of the juice.

2 Meanwhile, heat 4 small individual earthenware casseroles (*cazuelas*) either on the hob (see page 41 for instructions on tempering *cazuelas* to withstand direct heat) or in a preheated oven, 180°C (350°F), Gas Mark 4. Ladle in the soupy bread with its broth and crack in the eggs – one for each casserole. You can return them to the oven for the eggs to set, or serve immediately, for people to stir the egg into the boiling soup.

Shellfish Soup with Sherry

Sopa de mariscos con vino de Jerez

SERVES 4

500 g (1 lb) soup fish (or
ask your fishmonger
for bones and heads)

about 1 litre (1¾ pints)
water

about 200 ml (7 fl oz)
dry sherry

1 onion, quartered but
unpeeled

1 carrot, roughly
chopped

3–4 parsley sprigs

1–2 bay leaves

½ teaspoon crushed
peppercorns

12 saffron threads
soaked in 1 tablespoon
boiling water

1 kg (2 lb) live shellfish,
cleaned (see page 99)

1 tablespoon diced
serrano ham

1 tablespoon pimentón
(Spanish paprika)

salt and freshly milled
black pepper

1 teaspoon grated
lemon rind

1 teaspoon finely
chopped garlic

1 tablespoon chopped
parsley

You need fresh live shellfish on the shell for this dish – ready-cooked won't do. If this proves impossible, a combination of firm-fleshed white fish – monkfish, swordfish – and oysters gives good results. Shuck the oysters first, naturally, and slip them in right at the end to heat through.

1 Rinse the soup fish (or the bones and heads – if using the latter, be careful to remove the gills or the stock will become bitter) and transfer to a roomy saucepan with the water and sherry. Bring to the boil and skim off the foam. Add the onion, carrot, aromatics and 1 teaspoon salt. Return everything to the boil, turn the heat down immediately and simmer for 20 minutes – no longer or the broth will be bitter.

2 Strain the broth and return it to the pan. Stir in the saffron and its soaking water – first crushed either with the back of the spoon or given a quick whizz in a liquidizer.

3 Reheat to just boiling and add the shellfish, ham and pimentón. Return everything to the boil, cover and cook for about 3–4 minutes until the shellfish open. Discard any that remain closed. Remove from the heat and taste and adjust the seasoning. Finish by sprinkling over the lemon rind, garlic and parsley. Serve without reheating.

Scrambled Eggs with Mushrooms
Revuelto de setas

SERVES 3–4

4 tablespoons olive oil

1–2 garlic cloves, finely chopped

about 350 g (11½ oz) fresh woodland mushrooms, such as saffron milk caps, porcini, chanterelles or oysters, sliced

2 tablespoons diced serrano ham

6 free-range eggs

1 tablespoon finely chopped parsley

salt and freshly milled black pepper

Scrambling eggs with olive oil is the perfect way to stretch the gatherings of any firm-fleshed wild fungi. In spring, a fresh-flavoured revuelto *is made with asparagus sprue – chewy little green shoots gathered from beneath the prickly bushes of the native wild asparagus.*

1 Heat the oil in a flameproof earthenware casserole (*cazuela*) or a heavy iron frying pan and add the garlic. Allow to sizzle for a minute or two until the garlic softens, then add the mushrooms and ham. Sprinkle with a little salt and turn up the heat until the mushrooms absorb the oil. Turn down the heat and cook gently until the fungi yield up their juices, then begin to fry again.

2 Meanwhile, lightly beat the eggs with the parsley, and season with a little salt and plenty of pepper. Stir the eggs into the mushrooms and continue to stir over a gentle heat until the eggs form soft curds – no more than 1–2 minutes. Remove the cooking implement from the heat just before the egg sets. Stir again and serve in the cooking dish, with plenty of crusty bread for mopping.

Ham and Eggs with Red Peppers

Huevos al plato con pimientos

SERVES 4

2 garlic cloves, halved
2 red peppers
4 tablespoons olive oil
4 slices of serrano ham
8 free-range eggs
freshly milled black
  pepper

This makes an easy evening meal for townies who have been out on a tapa bar round with friends after work. Spaniards prefer to lunch prodigiously and take a relatively light supper.

1 For the proper presentation of this simple recipe, you will need 4 individual earthenware casseroles (*cazuelas*) that have been tempered to withstand direct heat. To temper, rub the surface inside and out with the garlic (the inside is glazed, the outside unglazed), fill the *cazuela* with water and place it over direct heat – gas or electric, or any open flame. Bring to the boil and boil steadily until the water has completely evaporated.

2 Roast the peppers whole by holding them over a gas or candle flame, speared on the end of a knife, or cook under a preheated hot grill, until the skin blisters and blackens.

3 Seal the peppers in a plastic food bag, wait 10 minutes for the skin to loosen, then peel with your fingers. Deseed and cut the flesh into strips.

4 Pour a tablespoon of oil into each individual *cazuela* and place them carefully on direct heat. When the oil is smoking hot, lay in the peppers and a slice of ham and crack in the eggs – 2 for each *cazuela*. Cook for 3–4 minutes to set the white. Give each dish a turn of the pepper mill and then serve. The eggs will continue to cook in their dish.

Potato Tortilla
Tortilla española

SERVES 4

about 750 g (1½ lb) potatoes (allow 1 medium potato per egg)

olive oil, for frying

1 tablespoon finely chopped onion

4 large free-range eggs

½ teaspoon salt

Call it egg and chips, Spanish-style: same ingredients, different method of attack. Opinions vary about the inclusion of parsley and onion; I leave the first one out and put the second one in. Some like the potatoes cut into thin rounds, others like them chip-shaped or cubed.

1 Peel and dice or slice the potatoes. Heat enough oil to submerge the potatoes completely – choose a frying pan in which you would usually cook a one-person omelette. Add the potatoes and fry gently until absolutely soft – don't let them colour. Add the onion for the last few minutes, just long enough to soften it.

2 Transfer the potato and onion to a sieve placed over a bowl to catch the drippings. Allow to cool to finger temperature. Lightly beat the eggs with the salt, then stir in the potatoes. At this point, the volume of the cooked potato should equal the volume of egg.

3 Pour all but a tablespoon of the oil out of the pan and add the drippings from the bowl (the rest of the oil can be used again). Reheat the pan and tip in the egg and potato mixture. Prod down the potato so that it's all submerged. Use a fork to pull the egg into the middle as soon as the edges begin to set. Fry gently, loosely lidded, until the surface no longer looks absolutely runny. The heat should be low or the base will burn before the egg is cooked. Don't overcook it – the centre should remain juicy. If the heat is too high, the egg will be leathery.

4 Place a clean plate over the pan and invert the whole thing with one quick movement so that the tortilla lands juicy-side up. Be brave: it's no harder than flipping a pancake. Reheat the pan with a little more oil and slip the tortilla, soft-side down, back into the pan and set the other side. When the underside is done, reverse the tortilla back on to the plate and pat off the excess oil with kitchen paper. Serve at room temperature, cut into neat wedges or cubes.

Chickpea and Chorizo Tortilla
Tortilla catalana

SERVES 4

2 tablespoons olive oil

2 tablespoons diced butifarra or chorizo

6 tablespoons cooked chickpeas, well drained

4 large free-range eggs

salt and freshly milled black pepper

This spicy winter tortilla is made with leftovers from the bean pot and a handful of diced butifarra negro – black pudding spiced with cinnamon, cloves and nutmeg. If you can't find butifarra, use chorizo. Haricot or butter beans can replace the chickpeas, depending on what's available.

1 Warm a tablespoon of the oil in a one-person omelette pan. Fry the sausage for a few minutes until the edges brown and the fat runs. Add the chickpeas and warm them through.

2 Beat the eggs lightly with salt and pepper. Mix in the contents of the omelette pan. Wipe the pan and heat the rest of the oil. Tip in the egg mixture, stir to blend the ingredients as the egg sets a little and cook gently until it takes the form of a thick pancake, loosely covered, neatening the side as the curds firm up.

3 Turn it by reversing the whole panful on to a plate so that the contents end up soft-side down. Slip it back into the hot pan (add a little more oil if necessary) to allow the other side to set – a couple of minutes. The whole operation should be very gentle and take no more than 7–8 minutes in all.

Scrambled Eggs with Vegetables
Piperrada

SERVES 4

4 tablespoons olive oil

1 onion, finely sliced into half-moons

1 garlic clove, finely chopped

1 aubergine, diced

1 red pepper, cored, deseeded and diced

1 large tomato, skinned, deseeded and chopped

4 free-range eggs, lightly beaten to blend

a little chilli powder

salt

In this speciality of the Basque Country, eggs are scrambled into a juicy combination of aubergine, tomato and garlic cooked in oil. The vegetables can be prepared ahead and the eggs scrambled at the last minute.

1 Heat half the oil in a flameproof earthenware casserole (*cazuela*) or heavy iron frying pan. Add the onion and garlic, salt lightly and cook very gently for at least 20 minutes until the onion slices soften and brown a little – don't let them burn. Remove to a sieve placed over a bowl to catch the drippings.

2 Reheat the pan with the remaining oil and add the aubergine. Cook until soft and lightly caramelized at the edges (return the drippings to the pan as soon as they are available). Remove the aubergine and reserve.

3 Add the red pepper and turn it in the hot oil until it has softened and taken a little colour. Add the tomato and bubble up for a minute or two until the flesh begins to collapse. Return the reserved vegetables to the pan and reheat. Season with salt and the chilli powder.

4 Fold the eggs into the vegetables and stir over a gentle heat while the eggs form soft curds – about 1–2 minutes, no more. Remove from the heat immediately.

5 If you like, serve with toasted country bread and a garlic clove for rubbing over the crisp crumb – this is a *campesino* dish, nothing fancy. One countryman can manage the whole thing; townies have more delicate appetites.

Meat & Poultry

Chicken with Garlic
Pollo al ajillo

SERVES 4

1 small free-range chicken, jointed into bite-sized pieces

1–2 tablespoons seasoned plain flour

about 8 tablespoons olive oil

8–12 garlic cloves, unpeeled

about 150 ml (¼ pint) dry sherry or white wine

This is the Andalusian housewife's way with a tender young chicken. Pick a small bird with a high ratio of bone to flesh – more chewable and easier to eat with fingers. The olive oil must be mild and golden, not leafy, which will taste bitter once subjected to high heat.

1 Dust the chicken joints through the seasoned flour.

2 Heat the oil in a heavy frying pan until a faint blue haze rises. Add the chicken joints, turn down the heat and fry gently for about 10 minutes, turning to brown all sides. Add the garlic cloves and fry them for about 5 minutes until the papery coverings brown a little.

3 Add the sherry or wine and allow to bubble up until the steam no longer smells winey. Turn down the heat and simmer gently for another 15 minutes, or until the chicken is cooked right through, the sherry or wine has completely evaporated and the juices are reduced to a thick, oily little dressing. To test the chicken for doneness, push a sharp knife through the thickest part of one of the thigh joints: when the juices run clear rather than pink, it's ready.

4 Allow to cool a little, then serve with chunks of country bread and eat it with your fingers.

Breaded Escalopes
Filete a la milanesa

SERVES 4

500 g (1 lb) veal, beef or
  pork escalopes

2 tablespoons seasoned
  plain flour

2 free-range eggs

2 tablespoons milk

4 heaped tablespoons
  fresh breadcrumbs

olive oil, for frying

1 lemon, quartered, to
  serve

Thrifty Spanish cooks would be lost without this easy way to make a little go a long way. There was a time when fresh meat, a luxury until modern and more prosperous times, was eaten only on Sundays, and even then only by city folk.

1 Place each escalope between 2 large sheets of clingfilm and flatten with a rolling pin. The meat should be extremely thin.

2 Spread the seasoned flour on one plate, beat the eggs and milk together on another and spread the breadcrumbs on a third. Dust the escalopes through the flour (shake off the excess), then flip them through the egg and milk to coat both sides. Press well into the breadcrumbs, making sure that both surfaces are well jacketed.

3 Heat a finger's depth of oil in a frying pan – you'll need just enough depth to submerge the meat. The oil should be hot but not yet smoking – test with a bread cube, which should form bubbles around the edges and become golden within a moment. Slip in the escalopes, 1–2 at a time so that the temperature doesn't drop. Turn to fry the other side. Transfer to kitchen paper to drain. Serve with the lemon quarters. Mashed potato, beaten with oil rather than butter and flavoured with ground allspice, is the perfect accompaniment.

Mincemeat with Saffron and Raisins
Picadillo valenciana

SERVES 4

750 g (1½ lb) minced
meat (best done by
hand with a knife, but
no matter)

1 tablespoon finely
diced serrano ham

2 tablespoons olive oil

1 large onion, diced

1 large carrot, diced

1 garlic clove, peeled

6–8 saffron threads

2 large ripe tomatoes,
skinned, deseeded
and diced, or 2
tablespoons tomato
purée

1 tablespoon raisins

500 g (1 lb) potatoes,
peeled and cut into
bite-sized cubes

½ teaspoon ground
cinnamon

1 bay leaf

salt and freshly milled
black pepper

TO GARNISH

1 tablespoon toasted
pine nuts

2 hard-boiled free-range
eggs, shelled and
quartered

*Moorish spicing and a touch of sweetness enlivens Monday's mince.
I loved this dish when I was a teenager in Madrid. My mother's cook
came from Valencia and included saffron, cinnamon and raisins
whenever she could. This is perfect spoon food for toothless grannies
and hungry children.*

1 Mix the minced meat with the ham. Heat the oil in
a flameproof casserole or heavy saucepan. When it is
good and hot, stir in the meat, onion and carrot and let
everything cook gently until it loses its water, begins to
fry and takes a little colour.

2 Meanwhile, crush the garlic and saffron with a little
salt, dilute with a splash of water and stir this paste into
the meat as soon as it begins to fry.

3 Add the tomatoes and bubble up until the flesh softens
and collapses or stir in the tomato purée. Add the raisins,
potatoes, cinnamon and bay leaf, and turn to blend with
the meat. Add enough water to just cover everything.

4 Bubble up again and turn down the heat. Cover loosely
and leave to simmer gently for 25–30 minutes, or until
the meat is tender and the potatoes are soft. Taste and
adjust the seasoning, turn up the heat and let it bubble
up to evaporate the extra moisture – it should be juicy
but not soupy.

5 To finish, scatter over the toasted pine nuts and hard-
boiled egg quarters.

Boned Stuffed Chicken
Galantina de gallina

SERVES 6–8

1 free-range chicken,
about 1.5 kg (3 lb)

450 g (14½ oz) minced
pork (choose a fatty
cut – shoulder or belly)

450 g (14½ oz) minced
veal or young beef

4 heaped tablespoons
fresh breadcrumbs

300 ml (½ pint) white
wine

2 free-range eggs, lightly
beaten

¼ teaspoon freshly
grated nutmeg

1 onion, quartered

1 large carrot, cut into
chunks

2–3 green celery sticks

1–2 bay leaves

½ teaspoon peppercorns

salt and freshly milled
black pepper

A poached stuffed chicken, eaten cold and served in much the same way as French pâté, is well worth the effort of boning out the bird. You'll find the commercially prepared version on the cold meats stall in Spanish markets, along with the serrano hams.

1 To bone out the chicken, lay the bird on its breast, back uppermost, and make a long slit with a sharp, slender-bladed knife right down the broad backbone. Ease the flesh from the skeleton as if opening a book, first one side and then the other, using the knife to separate the skin and flesh from the carcass. Pull the flesh up the legs, severing the skin where it joins the drumsticks. Trim off the wings at the second joint – no need to bone them out. Work your way up the carcass and over the breast, releasing the meat from the ribcage. Free the breastbone by slicing through the soft cartilage, keeping the skin intact.

2 Lay the boned-out chicken on the table with its flesh side uppermost. Remove most of the breast fillets and the thick leg meat. Chop this roughly and mix with the minced meats and breadcrumbs – enough to make a firm mixture. Moisten with 2–3 tablespoons of the wine, work in the eggs and then season with salt and pepper and the nutmeg.

3 Pat the mixture into a sausage shape and place on the boned-out chicken. How much you need depends on the meatiness of the bird (save any left over stuffing to fry as patties.) Re-form the casing over the stuffing and sew up the openings with a sturdy needle and strong thread. Wrap in a clean cloth and tie or sew to make a neat chicken-shaped bolster.

4 Place the bolster in a roomy flameproof pot just large enough to hold it comfortably. Add the remaining ingredients including the rest of the wine and some salt, and pour in enough water to submerge everything.

5 Bring to the boil, then turn down the heat, cover and leave to simmer very gently for 1½ hours or so until firm and cooked right through. Remove from the heat and leave to cool in its poaching water.

6 Once cooled, unwrap the gallatine and pack it into a loaf tin into which it will just fit. Weight down under a board and leave overnight in the refrigerator to firm and set. Cut into slices to serve, with a potato salad dressed with a homemade mayonnaise as a starter or light summer lunch.

Turkey with Red Peppers
Pavo chilindrón

SERVES 6

1 kg (2 lb) turkey meat, diced

2 garlic cloves, crushed

4 tablespoons olive oil

1 large mild onion, sliced into half-moons

6 red peppers, cored, deseeded and sliced into strips

1 tablespoon diced ham

500 g (1 lb) tomatoes, skinned and chopped

1 small cinnamon stick

about 200 ml (7 fl oz) red wine

a little sugar (optional)

salt and freshly milled black pepper

This is a classic dish from Saragossa in Aragón, where they grow particularly succulent red peppers. You can also make it with chicken or rabbit. If using turkey, the robust flavour of the leg meat is preferable to the softer flesh of the breast. A pretty dish for a party.

1 Fold the turkey meat with the garlic and season with salt and pepper.

2 Heat the oil in a roomy frying pan and fry the onion and peppers until they soften and take a little colour. Turn down the heat and cook very gently for 20 minutes or so until the water has evaporated and the vegetables are soft and thick.

3 Add the turkey meat and ham. Fry for 5–10 minutes until the meat seizes and takes a little colour. Add the tomatoes, cinnamon stick and wine and allow to bubble up until the steam no longer smells of alcohol.

4 Turn down the heat, cover tightly and simmer for 30–40 minutes – you may need to add a little more water if it looks like drying out – until the turkey meat is perfectly tender and the juices are well reduced. If it looks a little watery, remove the lid and let it bubble up fiercely for 1–2 minutes, or until the sauce is thick and shiny. Taste and adjust the seasoning – you might need a little sugar if the tomatoes were not particularly ripe. Bubble up for a few minutes more to marry the flavours.

5 Serve with white rice or plenty of bread. Good on the first day, better on the second.

Pasta Paella
Fideos a la catalana

SERVES 4

2 tablespoons olive oil

2 garlic cloves, chopped

2 tablespoons chopped parsley

1 tablespoon roughly chopped blanched almonds

about 150 ml (¼ pint) dry sherry or white wine

1 tablespoon pimentón (Spanish paprika)

1 teaspoon ground cinnamon

½ teaspoon ground cloves

12 saffron threads, soaked in 1 tablespoon boiling water

250 g (8 oz) dried pasta, such as small elbow macaroni, spaghettini broken into short lengths or thicker varieties of soup vermicelli

225 g (7½ oz) pork, diced

1 large onion, finely chopped

500 g (1 lb) tomatoes, skinned and chopped

300 ml (½ pint) water

salt

In this Catalan version of paella, rice is replaced by pasta of much the same volume and similar shape. Pork is the usual meat, but you can include prawns, shellfish, morcilla or chorizo. The almonds for the sauce, another strictly Catalan preparation, can be replaced by cubed bread.

1 Heat the oil in a frying pan and fry the garlic, parsley and almonds until the garlic and almonds are golden. Add the sherry or wine and allow to bubble up. Transfer all the solids to a food processor and process with the ground spices and saffron and its soaking water until you have a smooth paste, or pound in a mortar with a pestle. Reserve the oil.

2 In a paella pan or large frying pan, heat the reserved oil until a faint blue haze rises. Add the pasta and turn it in the hot oil until it takes a little colour.

3 Add the pork and onion, sprinkle with a little salt and continue to fry until the meat and the onion lose their water and begin to caramelize.

4 Add the tomatoes and the almond paste diluted with the water. Bubble up and cook gently until the meat is cooked through, the pasta is tender and the surface of the *fideu* is beginning to look dry rather than soupy. Add another splash of boiling water if it looks like drying out before the pasta is soft.

5 If you wish to eat in traditional style, serve as you would a paella, unplated but with forks for everyone to eat the portion in front of them.

Chicken with Almonds and Saffron
Pollo con almendras y azafràn

SERVES 4

1 free-range chicken
1.5 k (3 lb), jointed
into about 12 pieces

4 tablespoons pure pork
lard or olive oil

2 garlic cloves, chopped

1 thick slice of day-old
bread

1 tablespoon chopped
parsley

2 tablespoons ground
almonds

1 teaspoon ground
cinnamon

½ teaspoon ground
cloves

12 saffron threads,
soaked in 1 tablespoon
boiling water

juice and grated rind of
1 lemon

about 150 ml (¼ pint)
dry sherry or white
wine

1 large onion, finely
sliced

salt and freshly milled
black pepper

1 tablespoon toasted
flaked almonds, to
garnish (optional)

This dish of tender chicken cooked in a saffron sauce spiced with cinnamon and thickened with pounded almonds is from the days of the Moors.

1 Trim the chicken joints, removing any whiskery feathers and flaps of skin, and season with salt and pepper.

2 Heat half the lard or oil in a frying pan and fry the garlic and bread until both are golden. Add the parsley and fry for a moment longer.

3 Transfer the contents of the pan to a food processor and process briefly, or pound in a mortar with a pestle. Add the ground almonds, cinnamon and cloves, the saffron and its soaking water, lemon juice and rind and the sherry or wine. Continue to process to a smooth purée.

4 Meanwhile, reheat the pan and add the remaining lard or oil. Gently fry the onion and chicken joints until the skin has browned a little and the onion is soft and golden. Stir in the nut purée and allow to bubble up. Cover, turn down the heat and simmer gently until the chicken joints are cooked right through and the sauce is concentrated to a couple of spoonfuls – add a little boiling water only if needed. To test the chicken for doneness, push a sharp knife through the thickest part of one of the thigh joints: when the juices run clear rather than pink, it's ready. Taste and adjust the seasoning, if necessary.

5 Heap on a warm serving dish and sprinkle with toasted flaked almonds, if you like.

Grilled Steaks with Hazelnut Salsa
Chuletas de ternera a la parilla con salsa de avellanas

SERVES 4

4 beef or veal T-bone
  steaks

1–2 tablespoons olive
  oil

1 garlic clove, finely
  chopped

salt and freshly milled
  black pepper

SALSA

100 g (3½ oz) toasted
  hazelnuts (skinned or
  not, as you please)

1 shallot or small onion,
  roughly chopped

2 tablespoons cider
  vinegar

4 tablespoons finely
  chopped parsley

1 tablespoon water

4 tablespoons olive oil

dry crust of bread
  (optional)

*In the Basque Country, young thick beef steaks on the bone are
the great luxury, a taste that can only be satisfied by a trip to one
of the* asadores *that specialize in grilled meats and nothing else.
T-bone steaks cut from young beef come closest to the real thing.*

1 Wipe over the steaks and rub the surfaces with the
oil. Sprinkle with the garlic and season with salt and
pepper. Cover and leave for 1–2 hours at room
temperature to take the flavours.

2 Put all the salsa ingredients except the oil into a
liquidizer or food processor and process to a smooth
purée. Add the oil gradually in a thin stream, as if
making a mayonnaise, and process until you have
a creamy sauce. If it's a hot day, add a dry crust
of bread to maintain the emulsion.

3 Grill the meat on a preheated barbecue or under a
preheated grill over fierce heat, turning it once, until
done to your liking. To test for doneness, prod the meat
with your finger – if it feels soft, the meat will be rare;
if the surface still has a little elasticity, it will be medium
done; if firm, it's well done. To check, place your
forefinger on the tip of your thumb and feel the firmness
of the thumb ball; replace the forefinger with the second
finger and feel again, and so on until you reach the little
finger. The forefinger produces the softest thumb ball,
corresponding to meat cooked rare, and the little finger
produces the hardest, corresponding to well done.

4 Serve each steak with a thick slab of country bread and
hand round the salsa separately. Cider is the appropriate
accompaniment: this is apple country.

Quail with Parsley and Garlic Sauce
Codornices a la parilla con salsa verde

SERVES 4

8 quails

MARINADE

2 tablespoons olive oil

juice of 1 lemon

2 garlic cloves, finely
slivered

1 tablespoon dried
oregano

salt and freshly milled
black pepper

SAUCE

2 slices of country
bread, crusts
removed, soaked
in water and
squeezed dry

2 garlic cloves, roughly
crushed with a little
salt

2 handfuls or 300 ml
(½ pint) loosely-
packed flat leaf
parsley leaves,
chopped

2 tablespoons white
wine or sherry vinegar

150 ml (¼ pint) olive oil

Farmed quail, with their delicate, pale and tender meat inclined to blandness, take well to a robust parsley and garlic sauce from the Basque Country.

1 First spatchcock the quail. Split each carcass in half right down the back, open it out and press firmly on the breastbone to flatten – it'll look like a squashed frog but will cook in double-quick time.

2 Thread the quail on skewers to keep them spread out flat. Sprinkle both sides with the marinade ingredients. Cover and leave for 1–2 hours at room temperature or overnight in the refrigerator to take the flavours.

3 Cook the birds under a grill preheated to maximum heat, or roast in a preheated oven, 240°C (475°F), Gas Mark 9, for 10 minutes on one side. Turn, baste and allow another 5–8 minutes on the other side until the flesh is firm and the skin beautifully browned. Test by pushing a larding needle or fine skewer into the breast and thigh of one of the birds – the juices should run clear.

4 Meanwhile, make the sauce. Put all the ingredients except the oil in a liquidizer or food processor and process to a smooth purée. Add the oil gradually in a thin stream, as if making a mayonnaise, and process until you have a creamy sauce. If it splits, a splash of boiling water will bring it back.

5 Serve the birds with the sauce handed round separately. For a more substantial dish, place each bird on a thick slab of toasted country bread spread with the sauce.

Spiced Pork and Onion Pie
Empanada gallega

SERVES 4–6
FILLING

300 g (10 oz) lean pork, trimmed and diced

1 tablespoon pimentón (Spanish paprika)

½ tablespoon dried oregano

1 garlic clove, crushed

2 tablespoons olive oil

1 onion, diced

2 red peppers, cored, deseeded and diced

about 75 ml (3 fl oz) white wine

½ teaspoon saffron threads, soaked in 1 tablespoon boiling water

500 g (1 lb) tomatoes, skinned, deseeded and diced

1 tablespoon diced serrano ham or lean bacon

1 teaspoon dried thyme

2–3 anchovy fillets, chopped

½ teaspoon chilli flakes

salt (optional)

A juicy meat pie spiced with pimentón and baked between two layers of pastry makes excellent picnic food. This particular filling is typically Galician, other regions having their own versions. Although the pastry can be of your own choosing, a yeast pastry is more common in the region.

1 Make the pastry first. Sift the flour with the salt into a warm bowl and mix in the dried yeast. Make a well in the middle and pour in the warm water. Sprinkle the surface with a handful of flour and leave for 10 minutes in a warm place to allow the yeast to begin working. Add the oil (it should be as warm as your hand) and work the dry and wet ingredients together with the hook of your hand until you have soft, elastic dough. Drop the ball of dough back into the bowl, cover the bowl with clingfilm and set in a warm place for 1–2 hours until it has doubled in size.

2 Meanwhile, make the filling. Turn the pork in the pimentón, oregano and garlic. Heat half the oil in a frying pan and gently fry the meat until it stiffens and browns a little. Remove and reserve.

3 Reheat the pan with the remaining oil and fry the onion and peppers for at least 10 minutes until they soften. Add the wine, saffron and its soaking water, tomatoes, ham or bacon, thyme and anchovies. Bubble up for a moment.

4 Return the meat to the pan and let it bubble up again. Cover loosely and simmer for about 20 minutes, or until the liquid has evaporated and the meat is tender. Taste and add the chilli flakes and salt if necessary (the anchovies provide salt). Leave to cool while you finish the pastry.

5 Knock back the dough to distribute the air bubbles by punching it with your fist. Knead until elastic and springy – you'll feel the dough continue to rise as you work. Cut the dough into 2 pieces, one a little larger than the other. Brush a baking tray (about 34 x 22 cm/13½ x 8½ inches) with oil and dust with a little flour (nonstick needs no such attention). Work each piece of dough into a smooth ball.

6 On a floured surface, pat out or roll each ball to form 2 rectangles, one roughly the same size as the baking tray, the other a little smaller. Lay the larger piece in the baking tray, bringing it comfortably up the sides. Spread the filling over the pastry in an even layer. Dampen the edges of the pastry and top with the remaining dough. Work the 2 edges together in a rope pattern with a damp finger. Prick the top in a few places with a fork and paint with beaten egg to give the pie a pretty glaze.

7 Place in a preheated oven, 180°C (350°F), Gas Mark 4, for 40–50 minutes, or until the pastry is well risen and browned. Serve at room temperature.

PASTRY

300 g (10 oz) strong bread flour, plus extra for dusting

½ teaspoon salt

1 teaspoon easy-blend dried yeast

150 ml (¼ pint) warm water

4 tablespoons oil, plus extra for oiling

beaten egg, to glaze

Pot-roast Lamb with Almonds
Cordero estofado en salsa de almendras

SERVES 4

1.5 kg (3 lb) thick lamb steaks (shoulder or leg), chopped right across the bone

200 g (7 oz) whole unblanched almonds

4 tablespoons olive oil

1 whole head of garlic (about 12 cloves), cloves separated but not peeled

1–2 bay leaves

1 thyme sprig

200 ml (7 fl oz) white wine or dry sherry

200 ml (7 fl oz) water

1 tablespoon pimentón (Spanish paprika), preferably smoked

salt and freshly milled black pepper

1 tablespoon toasted flaked almonds (optional)

In this recipe from the shepherding regions of Spain (anywhere north of Andalusia), lamb on the bone is flavoured with garlic and finished with a thick paste of toasted almonds and pimentón. In the south, where the goat is the usual milk animal, it's made with kid.

1 Wipe over the lamb and season with salt and pepper.

2 Toast the almonds gently in a heavy, flameproof earthenware or enamel casserole with a teaspoon of the oil. As soon as the skins loosen and the nuts begin to brown, remove and set aside.

3 Reheat the casserole with the remaining oil and fry the meat, turning to brown all sides. Add the garlic cloves and fry for another few minutes. Add the herbs, wine or sherry and the water, and allow to bubble up.

4 Turn down the heat and leave to simmer gently, loosely covered, for 1 hour until the meat is tender enough to eat with a spoon. Alternatively, place in a preheated oven, 160°C (325°F), Gas Mark 3, for the same amount of time. Check occasionally and add another glassful of water if necessary. The cooking broth should be well reduced by the end, but the meat should never be allowed to dry out.

5 Remove a spoonful of the broth, put it with the reserved almonds and pimentón into a liquidizer and process to a paste, or pound in a mortar with a pestle. Stir the paste into the cooking juices and bubble up again to thicken.

6 Heap everything on to a warm serving dish and scatter with the toasted flaked almonds, if you like.

Braised Lamb Shanks
Caldereta de piernas de cordero

SERVES 4

4 lamb shanks

2 tablespoons olive oil

1 tablespoon diced serrano ham or lean bacon

250 g (8 oz) small shallots or baby onions

1 large carrot, cut into chunks

500 g (1 lb) ripe tomatoes, skinned, deseeded and diced

2–3 garlic cloves, crushed with a little salt

1–2 rosemary sprigs

1–2 thyme sprigs

½ teaspoon peppercorns, crushed

about 200 ml (7 fl oz) dry sherry or white wine

salt

The shank – the end piece of the shoulder – cooks to a gluey softness when subject to gentle braising. Although the cooking time is long, the preparation is short – slow food at its most succulent. You can even leave it, tightly covered, in a low oven overnight.

1 Wipe over the lamb shanks and season with salt.

2 Heat the oil in a roomy, flameproof earthenware or enamel casserole that will just accommodate the lamb shanks in a single layer. Brown the meat lightly, turning to sear on all sides. Settle the shanks bone-end upwards.

3 Add the remaining ingredients, packing them around the sides of the casserole. Bring all to the boil, cover tightly (seal with a layer of foil, shiny-side downwards, if you're uncertain about the fit) and place in a preheated oven, 150°C (300°F), Gas Mark 2, for at least 3 hours – longer if that's more convenient – without unsealing, unless your nose and ears tell you that the meat is beginning to fry, when you'll need to add a splash of water. The meat should be tender enough to eat with a spoon and the sauce reduced to a thick jammy slick – very delicious indeed.

Wild Duck with Olives and Oranges
Pato a la sevillana

SERVES 4

2 mallard, quartered,
 or 4 smaller wild
 duck, halved

2 tablespoons olive oil

2 garlic cloves, finely
 chopped

2 tablespoons diced
 serrano ham

1 teaspoon ground
 cinnamon

½ teaspoon ground
 cloves

1 tablespoon green
 olives, pitted or not
 as you please

2 Seville oranges or
 small, thin-skinned
 lemons, diced

about 150 ml (¼ pint)
 dry sherry or white
 wine

salt (optional) and
 freshly milled black
 pepper

The wetlands of the Guadalquivir and Valencia attract all manner of overwintering duck, an attraction for the hunters. If you prefer, make this with a domestic duck, quartered. Seville oranges, thin-skinned and sharp, are available only in January and February; other times of the year use lemons or limes.

1 Wipe the duck joints and season with pepper. Trickle with half the oil and sprinkle with the garlic. Cover and leave for about 30 minutes at room temperature to take the flavours.

2 Heat the remaining oil in a heavy flameproof casserole and gently fry the duck joints until the skin takes a little colour. Add the ham, spices, olives and citrus fruit and turn over the heat for 1–2 minutes.

3 Pour in the sherry or wine and just enough water to cover and allow to bubble up. Cover loosely, turn down the heat and leave to simmer gently for 30–40 minutes, or until the birds are perfectly tender and the sauce reduced to a thick, rich citrus sludge.

4 Taste and add salt if necessary (the ham and olives are already salty) before serving. The duck is good accompanied by crisp twice-fried chips cooked in olive oil and a salad of curly endive tossed, as they like it in Seville, with a little sherry vinegar, olive oil, coarse salt and a few sprigs of tarragon.

Spiced Oxtail Hotpot
Estofado de rabo de buey

SERVES 4–6

1–2 oxtails (depending on size), cut into sections

2 tablespoons olive oil

1 tablespoon diced serrano ham or lean bacon

1 large onion, diced

2 garlic cloves, crushed with a little salt

1 green celery stick, chopped

1 large carrot, scrubbed and diced

500 g (1 lb) ripe tomatoes, skinned, deseeded and diced

1 tablespoon hot pimentón (Spanish chilli powder)

1 small cinnamon stick

½ teaspoon crushed allspice berries

3–4 cloves

1 bay leaf

1 bottle red wine

handful of cooked chickpeas (optional)

salt and freshly milled black pepper

Oxtail dishes are found in Spain wherever there was once leather-working, since the skins came with the tail still attached. This delicious version, perfumed with the spices beloved by the Moors, is how they like it in the city of Cordova, famed for hand-tooled leather since the days when Andalusia was ruled from Baghdad.

1 Rinse the oxtail and trim off the excess fat.

2 Heat the oil in a flameproof casserole that is large enough to comfortably accommodate all the pieces. Turn the oxtail pieces in the hot oil until the edges brown a little. Remove from the casserole. Add the ham or bacon, onion, garlic, celery and carrot to the casserole and fry gently until the vegetables soften. Add the tomatoes, spices and bay leaf and allow to bubble up to soften the tomatoes. Add the red wine and bubble up again until the steam no longer smells winey.

3 Return the oxtail to the pot and add enough water to barely cover all the pieces. Season with salt and pepper. Bring back to the boil, then turn down the heat, cover tightly and place in a preheated oven, 150°C (300°F), Gas Mark 2, for 3–4 hours, or until the meat is falling off the bones (or leave to cook on the hob on a very low heat). Check from time to time and add more water if necessary.

4 To finish, transfer the oxtail to a warm serving dish and bubble up the juices in the pot to concentrate the flavour. Check the seasoning. You can, if you like, stir in a ladleful of cooked chickpeas to make the oxtail go further. Good today, even better tomorrow.

Liver and Onions
Higado encebollado

SERVES 4

500 g (1 lb) veal liver,
finely sliced

1–2 tablespoons milk

4 tablespoons pure pork
lard or butter

500 g (1 lb) onions, finely
sliced

1 heaped tablespoon
seasoned plain flour

½ teaspoon fennel seeds

salt and freshly milled
black pepper

Here, a great deal of onion makes a sauce for the tender meat, which is cooked rare. This is a classic combination from the Basque Country, very simple and very good.

1 Cut the liver into fine strips and leave it to soak in the milk for 30 minutes.

2 Heat 3 tablespoons of the lard or butter in a heavy frying pan. Add the onions, salt lightly and let them cook very slowly for 25–30 minutes, turning them regularly, until soft and lightly caramelized. Remove to a sieve placed over a bowl to catch the drippings.

3 Drain the liver strips and flip them quickly through the seasoned flour. Reheat the pan with the remaining lard or butter and the drippings from the bowl. Drop in the liver and sear the strips briefly but fiercely, shaking the pan so that the heat reaches all sides, allowing no more than a couple of minutes.

4 Return the onions to the pan and sprinkle with the fennel seeds. Turn to blend the onion and the meat and cook gently for another 5 minutes to blend the flavours. Taste and adjust the seasoning. That's all.

Rabbit with Prunes
Conejo con ciruelas pasas

SERVES 4-6

- 1 large rabbit (2 if wild and small), jointed
- 2 tablespoons seasoned plain flour
- 2 tablespoons pure pork lard or butter
- 250 g (8 oz) small onions or shallots
- 3–4 garlic cloves, roughly chopped
- 300 ml (½ pint) red wine
- 1 thyme sprig
- 1–2 bay leaves
- 2–3 cloves
- 1 short cinnamon stick
- 250 g (8 oz) prunes, soaked to swell
- salt and freshly milled black pepper

A recipe from the Basque Country, where rabbits fatten in the orchards and plums are dried for winter stores, this works almost as well with duck or chicken. If you should have any pacharán, Basque plum brandy, add a splash at the end and set it alight to burn off the alcohol.

1 If preparing the rabbit yourself, don't forget to lift off the bluish membrane that covers the back and legs, using a sharp knife, or the meat will never be tender. Dust the rabbit joints through the seasoned flour.

2 Heat the lard or butter in a roomy flameproof casserole and fry the onions or shallots and garlic gently until they take a little colour. Push to one side, then turn the rabbit joints in the hot fat and let them brown a little.

3 Add the wine, herbs and spices and a glass or two of water – just enough to cover everything. Allow to bubble up, turn down the heat and cover loosely. Leave to simmer gently for an hour until the meat is perfectly tender. Check every now and then in case you need to top up with a little more water.

4 After 30 minutes, add the prunes. Remove the lid at the end and bubble up to reduce the juices to a shiny little sauce. Taste and adjust the seasoning.

5 Serve in the cooking dish, or pile everything on a warm serving platter. Eat with a spoon and use your fingers – no one can eat a bony little rabbit with a knife and fork.

Chickpea and Chicken Stew
Puchero andaluz

SERVES 4−6

500 g (1 lb) dried chickpeas, soaked overnight

½ head of garlic (about 6 cloves)

1 short length of ham bone or bacon knuckle

2 free-range chicken quarters (a boiling fowl is best, a chicken will do)

1 bay leaf

½ teaspoon coriander seeds

6–8 black peppercorns

1 onion, roughly chopped

1 bay leaf

1 marjoram sprig

1–2 large potatoes, peeled and cut into bite-sized pieces

generous handful of spinach or chard leaves, shredded

2 tablespoons olive oil

salt

Spain's pucheros *and* cocidos *– generic names for anything that combines pulses with a scrap of meat or bones and is cooked in a boiling pot – have their origin in Moorish Andalusia. The dish is now naturalized throughout the land, each region having its own particular recipe.*

1 Drain the chickpeas and put them into a saucepan of water. Bring to the boil and skim off the grey foam that rises to the surface.

2 Spear the garlic head on a knife and hold over a gas or candle flame until the paper skin singes and blackens a little and the flesh is lightly caramelized. Drop it into the chickpea pan with the ham bone or bacon knuckle, chicken quarters, bay leaf, coriander seeds and peppercorns. Add the onion and herbs, but no salt.

3 Bring to the boil, then turn down the heat. Cover and cook for 1½–3 hours, or until the chickpeas are quite soft.

4 Keep the soup at a gentle boil – don't let the temperature drop or add salt, otherwise the chickpeas never seem to soften. If you need to add water, make sure it is boiling.

5 Thirty minutes before the end of cooking, add the potatoes. Ten minutes before the end, stir in the spinach or chard. Just before you are ready to serve, add salt and stir in the oil.

6 Serve in deep plates, accompanied by plenty of bread and a cos lettuce and onion salad on the side, if you like.

Bean Pot with Chorizo, Chicken and Beef
Olla podrida

SERVES 6−8

750 g (1½ lb) dried haricot beans, soaked overnight in cold water

½ head of garlic (6 cloves)

1 short length of serrano ham bone or bacon knuckle

5 tablespoons olive oil

1−2 bay leaves

2 dried red peppers, deseeded and torn, or 1 fresh red pepper, deseeded and sliced

½ teaspoon peppercorns, crushed

1 small free-range chicken about 1.5 kg (3 lb) (an old hen has the best flavour, a young one will do)

750 g (1½ lb) stewing beef in a single piece (preferably shin)

500 g (1 lb) pork belly, salted or fresh

1−2 carrots, chopped

1 onion, stuck with 2−3 cloves

250 g (8 oz) chorizo

250 g (8 oz) morcilla or black pudding

1 large sweet potato, peeled and cut into chunks

1 small green cabbage

2 green apples, peeled, cored and cut into chunks

salt and freshly milled black pepper

This is the stupendous bean pot as served in Madrid, which is as extravagant as can be expected from the nation's political capital, and is just as variable in its notions of what's acceptable. Chickpeas are traditional, but this version is based on white haricot beans.

1 Drain the beans, put them in a heavy saucepan and pour in enough cold water to submerge them to a depth of 2 fingers. Bring to the boil and skim off the grey foam that rises to the surface.

2 Spear the garlic head on a knife and hold over a gas or candle flame until the paper skin singes and blackens a little and the flesh is lightly caramelized. Drop it into the bean pot along with the ham bone or bacon knuckle, 4 tablespoons of the oil, bay leaves, red peppers and peppercorns. Bring all to the boil, and then turn down to a fast simmer. Cover loosely and leave to bubble gently, adding boiling water during the course of the cooking when needed. Beans are variable in the length of time they need to soften and can take anything from 1−3 hours to cook.

3 Meanwhile, put the chicken, beef and pork in another saucepan with the carrots and the onion stuck with the cloves and add enough water to submerge all completely. Season with salt and pepper. Bring to the boil, skim off the grey foam that rises to the surface and turn down the heat. Cover loosely and leave to simmer until all is tender.

4 In a small saucepan, make the tomato sauce: fry the onion gently in the oil until it softens and browns a little, then add the tomatoes. Allow to bubble up and then squash down with a fork until you have a thick, shiny deep red sauce. Season and reserve.

5 When the beans are soft but not yet mushy, add the chorizo, morcilla or black pudding and sweet potato. Bubble up again and turn down the heat to a simmer. Test for doneness after 20 minutes.

6 Meanwhile, prepare the cabbage: with a sharp knife, nick out the hard centre of the core, then slice thickly, making sure that each slice is held together by a strip of stalk. Pack the cabbage slices in a roomy saucepan and add a couple of ladlefuls of broth from the meats. Bring to the boil and drop in the apples. Cover tightly and cook for about 5 minutes until tender but still bright green.

7 Taste and add salt (if you have used salt pork it will have contributed to the saltiness), then stir in the remaining oil. Remove the chorizo and morcilla from the bean pot and heap them on a serving dish with the meats from the other pot. Moisten with cooking broth. Heap the meats, vegetables and beans in separate piles on another serving plate.

8 Serve the bean broth combined with the meat broth first in deep plates in which you may, if you like, place a slice of toasted bread rubbed with garlic, then serve the real food – beans, meats and vegetables including the cabbage and apples – as a second course. Serve the tomato sauce separately.

TOMATO SAUCE

1 onion, diced

2 tablespoons olive oil

1 kg (2 lb) ripe tomatoes, skinned and chopped

Venison Stewed with Chocolate
Venado estofado con chocolate

SERVES 4

1 kg (2 lb) shoulder
venison, diced

2 tablespoons oil

1 thick slice of serrano
ham fat or fatty
bacon, cubed

500 g (1 lb) baby onions
or shallots

1 large carrot, diced

plain flour, for dusting
(optional)

50 g (2 oz) bitter dark
chocolate, grated

1 tablespoon flaked
almonds

salt and freshly milled
black pepper

MARINADE

1 bottle red wine

2 tablespoons olive oil

1 tablespoon sherry or
red wine vinegar

2 garlic cloves, crushed

1–2 bay leaves

1 teaspoon crushed
allspice berries

½ teaspoon crushed
peppercorns

½ teaspoon salt

*Furry game is always improved by a night in a marinade: the meat is
invariably lean and dry, and the flavours must be well developed to be
convincing. The chocolate is used at the end to thicken and darken the
sauce, much as blood does if making a civet.*

1 Put the diced venison in a bowl and cover with the
marinade ingredients, turning to blend. Cover and leave
overnight in a cool place – 2 days is even better.

2 Next day, remove the venison from the marinade, drain
and shake dry, reserving the marinade.

3 Heat a tablespoon of the oil in a deep saucepan and
add the ham fat or bacon, half the onions or shallots and
the carrot. Let everything fry for a few minutes, then push
it all to one side and add the meat (you can dust the pieces
with flour first if you want a thicker sauce). Let the meat
seize and brown a little in the hot oil.

4 Add the marinade with all its bits, allow everything to
bubble up and then turn down the heat. Leave to simmer
gently, loosely covered, for an hour or so until the venison
is quite tender. You may need to add a little water – not
too much since you want a thick, rich sauce. Ten minutes
before end of the cooking, stir in the grated chocolate and
bubble up to blend and thicken. Taste and adjust the
seasoning if necessary.

5 Meanwhile, cook the remaining onions or shallots gently
in a closed pan with the remaining oil until they are golden
and tender, then remove and reserve. Fry the almonds
gently in the pan drippings until golden.

6 Heap the meat on a warm serving dish, spoon over the
sauce and finish with the onions or shallots and almonds.

Braised Veal with Serrano Ham
Guiso de ternera mechada

SERVES 6−8

2 kg (4 lb) boned-out
veal or young beef,
rolled and tied as for
a pot-roast

50 g (2 oz) thick-cut
serrano ham with
plenty of golden fat

500 g (1 lb) mature
carrots

4 tablespoons olive oil

500 g (1 lb) shallots or
baby onions

4 garlic cloves, crushed
with a little salt

125 g (4 oz) fresh
mushrooms (wild is
best), sliced

a few thyme and
oregano sprigs

1 bay leaf

½ teaspoon crushed
black pepper

¼ teaspoon crushed
allspice berries

1 bottle red wine

a little sugar

salt

*In Spain, veal is usually young beef rather than milk-fed calf, and is
naturally dry and mild flavoured. It benefits from larding – threading
the meat with strips of fatty pork or some other meat – which adds
richness and flavour.*

1 Insert a sharp knife right through the heart of the joint
to make a deep incision from end to end – starting at the
blunt end, the knife point should appear at the tip. Cut
the ham into matchsticks and cut one of the carrots into
narrow batons. Push the ham and carrot batons into the
incisions of the joint – be patient and use a skewer or
larding needle to help you on your way.

2 Heat the oil in a roomy flameproof casserole and brown
the meat on all sides. Pack in the shallots or onions, garlic
and remaining carrots, cut into chunks the same size as
the shallots or onions. Add the mushrooms.

3 Tuck in the herbs (in a little bunch, if that's convenient)
and the spices. Add the wine and season with salt and the
sugar to balance the acidity of the wine.

4 Bring to the boil, remove from the heat and cover
tightly – use foil as well as a lid. Place the casserole in a
preheated oven, 150°C (300°F), Gas Mark 2, and leave to
cook gently in its own juices for 2–3 hours – overnight is
not too long, although if this is your choice, you should
drop the temperature to 140°C (275°F), Gas Mark 1.

5 When the meat is perfectly tender, remove and leave to
rest before slicing. Serve at room temperature, with its sauce.

Butter Beans with Pork

Fabada asturiana

SERVES 6−8

750 g (1½ lb) smallish
dried butter beans,
soaked overnight in
cold water

½ head of garlic

1 large carrot, diced

2 small turnips, peeled
and diced

2 celery sticks, diced

500 g (1 lb) pork spare
rib

250 g (8 oz) chorizo

250 g (8 oz) morcilla or
black pudding
(optional)

sea salt and freshly
milled black pepper

TO GARNISH

chopped parsley

½ onion, finely chopped

*The Asturians – dairy-herding upland farmers with a tradition of
self-sufficiency – prefer the Peruvian native bean, the butter bean, to
the other storable beans. Not only does it thrive in the cold climate of
the highest mountain range in Spain but it also melts to a comforting
creaminess in a stew.*

1 Drain the beans and rinse them. Put them in a soup pot
with the rest of the ingredients and enough water to cover
them to a depth of 2 fingers. No salt yet.

2 Bring to the boil and then turn down to a simmer.
Cover loosely and leave to bubble gently for 1–2 hours,
or until the beans are perfectly soft and the meats tender
enough to eat with a spoon. Season with salt and pepper.

3 Serve in deep soup plates. If you like, hand round a
bowl of chopped parsley and raw onion for people to
add their own.

Fish & Shellfish

Catalan Fish Soup
Zarzuela catalana

SERVES 4 AS A
MAIN DISH

**500 g (1 lb) monkfish
tail, filleted**

**500 g (1 lb) sea bream,
filleted**

**350 g (11½ oz) squid,
cleaned (see page 94)**

**500 g (1 lb) live mussels,
cleaned (see page 99)**

500 ml (17 fl oz) water

**2–3 tablespoons
seasoned plain flour**

100 ml (3½ fl oz) olive oil

**1 small onion, finely
sliced**

**2 garlic cloves, finely
slivered**

**500 g (1 lb) ripe
tomatoes, skinned,
deseeded and diced**

1 short cinnamon stick

**about 12 saffron threads,
lightly toasted in a
dry pan**

**about 150 ml (¼ pint)
dry sherry or white
wine**

**12 large raw unpeeled
prawns or langoustines**

**salt and freshly milled
black pepper**

**2 tablespoons chopped
parsley, to garnish**

*This is the Catalan version of Provence's bouillabaisse, a member
of that venerable tribe of traditional Mediterranean fish soups that
makes the most of whatever comes to hand. These delicious one-pot
stews remain popular, their content becoming grander all the time.*

1 Chop the fish fillets into bite-sized pieces and slice the
squid into rings, leaving the tentacles in a bunch. Set aside.
Put the mussels in a roomy saucepan with the water, lightly
salted. Bring to the boil, cover and cook for 5 minutes or so
until the shells open.

2 Remove the pan from the heat and transfer the mussels
with a slotted spoon to a warm serving dish. Discard any
that remain closed. Strain the broth through a cloth-lined
sieve – mussels are hard to rid of all their sand – and reserve.

3 Place the seasoned flour on a plate and dust through the
fish pieces. Heat the oil in a roomy frying pan and fry the
floured fish for 2–3 minutes on each side until firm and
golden. Transfer to the serving dish with the mussels.

4 Reheat the pan and gently fry the onion and garlic until
they soften – don't let them brown. Add the tomatoes,
cinnamon stick and saffron and bubble up for a few minutes
until the tomato softens, mashing down to make a thick
sauce. Add the sherry or wine and bubble up to evaporate
the alcohol. Add the mussel broth and bubble up, stirring
to blend. Taste and season with pepper – you probably
won't need more salt.

5 Lay the prawns or langoustines in the hot broth. Allow
to bubble up and cook briefly until they turn opaque.
Transfer to the serving dish. Bubble up the sauce again
until thick and rich. Ladle the sauce over the fish and finish
with a generous shower of parsley.

Seafood Paella
Paella marinera

knife tip of saffron
threads (12–18), lightly
toasted in a dry pan

4 large ripe tomatoes

6–8 tablespoons olive oil

4 garlic cloves, unpeeled
and roughly chopped

1 rabbit (or 1 small
chicken), jointed into
16–20 bite-sized
pieces

500 g (1 lb) paella or
risotto rice (although
pudding rice will do)

handful of thin green
asparagus (sprue) or
young green beans,
chopped

1 kg (2 lb) live clams
and mussels, cleaned
(see page 99)

250 g (8 oz) unpeeled
prawns (freshwater
crayfish ideally)

salt and freshly milled
black pepper

A paella is traditionally prepared over a campfire in the open air, though Spanish cooks have access to a specially-wide gas ring which does the job just as well. Failing this, light a barbecue and let the coals die down to an even heat.

1 You'll need a 7-person paella pan, 45 cm/17¾ inches in diameter, and a heat source to match. In order for the rice to cook evenly in a single layer, the pan requires an even bed of heat that allows the full expanse of metal to come into contact with the heat source. If this is not available, use a large frying pan and remember to stir the rice as it cooks.

2 Put the saffron to soak in a splash of boiling water for 15 minutes or so. Meanwhile, grate the flesh of the tomatoes: cut each tomato through its equator and empty out the seeds. Holding the skin side firmly in your palm, rub the cut side through the coarse holes of the grater on to a plate. You should be left with an emptied-out shell in your hand and a juicy heap of pulp on the plate.

3 Set the pan on the fire and wait until it is hot. Preheating the pan avoids food sticking later. Add the oil and wait until it smokes. Immediately add the garlic and the jointed rabbit (or chicken) and turn the pieces over the heat. Cook gently until tender and no longer pink, turning regularly – this will take at least 20 minutes.

4 Add the rice and stir until all the grains are coated and transparent. Stir the tomato pulp into the rice. Add the saffron and its soaking water and top up with as much water as will cover the layer of rice to a depth of one finger – the liquid should be level with the screws that fix the handles to the pan. Allow all to bubble up, season with salt and pepper and leave to cook for 15–18 minutes.

Move the pan over the heat and add more water when necessary, but don't stir again. After 10 minutes, add the asparagus or green beans and the shellfish – the clams and mussels will open in the steam. Discard any shells that remain closed.

5 When it's ready, most of the liquid will have evaporated and little craters, like worm holes, will begin to appear on the surface. Test the rice for doneness by biting into a grain – it should be soft but still retain a nutty little heart.

6 Remove the pan from the heat, cover with a clean cloth or a couple of sheets of newspaper and leave for 10 minutes to allow the rice to finish swelling. A paella should be moist and succulent, never dry.

7 Settle everyone in a circle around the pan. Traditionally you should eat the portion in front of you straight from the pan. You may use clean fingers, or a spoon or lettuce leaves for scooping. Provide plenty of robust country bread for the faint-hearted who would otherwise go hungry.

Cuttlefish with Broad Beans
Sepia con habas

SERVES 4−6

1 kg (2 lb) whole squid
or cuttlefish

2 tablespoons olive oil

2 garlic cloves, finely
sliced

250 g (8 oz) shelled,
skinned broad beans

about 150 ml (¼ pint)
dry sherry

about 150 ml (¼ pint)
water

1 teaspoon marjoram
or oregano leaves

salt and freshly milled
black pepper

The creamy chewiness of the fish marries perfectly with the tender greenness of the beans. Squid can be substituted for the cuttlefish, and white beans – the large, floury pochas or the smaller kidney-shaped habichuelas *– can replace the broad beans.*

1 Rinse the squid or cuttlefish. Remove the bone (a long sheet of clear plastic in the squid; a chalky oval disc in the cuttlefish) and the soft innards with the tentacles and body attached. Discard the innards and the eye portion as well as the hard little beak-like mouthpiece. Slice the body and remaining head parts into rings. Rinse the tentacles in water and scrape off the little 'toenails'. If large, divide the tentacles into singles; if small, the tentacles look pretty left in their bunches.

2 Heat the oil gently in a flameproof casserole. Add the garlic and let it soften but not take on any colour. Add the fish and let it cook very gently for about 10 minutes until it yields up its juices.

3 Add the beans, sherry and the water and let it all bubble up. Sprinkle in the marjoram or oregano and season with pepper. Turn down the heat, cover loosely and leave to simmer for about 20–30 minutes, or until the beans and fish are tender.

4 Remove the lid, turn up the heat and bubble up to reduce the juices to an oily sauce. Taste and add salt. Serve with chunks of robust country bread for mopping.

Octopus with Onions and Potatoes

Pulpo encebollado con patatas

SERVES 4

1 smallish octopus, about 1 kg (2 lb), ready-cleaned

4 tablespoons olive oil

2 large onions, thinly sliced

1 tablespoon chopped parsley

about 12 saffron threads, soaked in 1 tablespoon boiling water

500 g (1 lb) yellow-fleshed potatoes, peeled and sliced

hot pimentón (Spanish chilli powder) or chilli flakes, to taste

salt

Octopus must be tenderized by bashing it thoroughly before you cook it – fishermen say to throw it 40 times against the rocks until the tentacles curl. Older specimens need lengthier tenderizing than young ones. Make it easy for yourself and pop it in the freezer for 48 hours.

1 Rinse the octopus and slice it into bite-sized pieces.

2 Heat the oil in a roomy frying pan and fry the onions very gently for 10 minutes until soft and golden – salt lightly to get the juices running.

3 Add the parsley and the saffron with its soaking water and allow to bubble up. Add the octopus and cook gently in its own juices (these are copious), loosely covered, for an hour. You may need to add a little water.

4 When the octopus is tender, add the potatoes, make sure that there's enough liquid to cover and continue to cook for another 15 minutes or so until the potatoes are perfectly tender. Taste and season with salt and hot pimentón or chilli flakes.

5 Serve the octopus in deep bowls, sauced with its own lovely juices.

Two-dish Rice
Arroz abanda

SERVES 6

1.5 litres (2½ pints)
   water

1 thyme sprig

1 bay leaf

about 150 ml (¼ pint)
   white wine

8 tablespoons olive oil

1 kg (2 lb) mixed fish
   fillets, divided into
   firm-fleshed and
   soft-fleshed

handful each of raw
   peeled prawns, live
   mussels and clams,
   cleaned (see page 99),
   (optional)

2 garlic cloves

2 tablespoons pimentón
   (Spanish paprika) or
   the pulp from 2 dried
   red peppers, soaked
   to soften

1 teaspoon salt

about 12 saffron threads,
   toasted in a dry pan

2 tablespoons chopped
   parsley

500 g (1 lb) paella or
   risotto rice

500 g (1 lb) tomatoes,
   skinned, deseeded
   and diced

ALIOLI

6 garlic cloves, crushed

1 teaspoon sea salt

about 300 ml (½ pint)
   extra-virgin olive oil

This is one of the two great rice dishes of the Levant – the other is paella – for which the rice and seafood are served separately. The firm-fleshed fish (monkfish, conger eel and weever fish are most favoured) and soft-fleshed fish (mackerel, bream and gallo, a Mediterranean plaice) are cooked in separate batches.

1 Bring the water to the boil in a roomy saucepan with the herbs, wine and half the oil. Add the firm-fleshed fish and bring back to the boil. Turn down the heat and leave to simmer for 5 minutes.

2 Add the soft-fleshed fish and prawns and shellfish, if using, and cook for a further 10 minutes. Carefully lift out the seafood and keep warm. Strain the fish stock and reserve.

3 Pound the garlic, pimentón or soaked peppers and salt in a mortar with a pestle. Heat the remainder of the oil in a paella pan – a large frying pan will do – add the garlic mixture, saffron and parsley and fry gently for a few minutes until the garlic softens.

4 Add the rice and turn it in the hot oil for a moment. Add the tomatoes and 1 litre (1¾ pints) of the fish stock – the volume of stock should be double that of the rice. Bring to the boil and let it bubble fiercely for 5 minutes, then turn down the heat and simmer for another 12 minutes. Add a little more fish stock as it dries out. Leave it to rest for 10–15 minutes after you take it off the heat. The rice should be juicy but with the grains visibly separate.

5 Meanwhile, to make the alioli, pound the garlic with the salt in a mortar with a pestle. Slowly trickle in the oil, working the paste so that the garlic acts like an emulsifier to make a rich, spoonable sauce for the fish.

6 Serve the sauce with the fish and shellfish. By the time the fish has all been eaten, the rice will be ready. The traditional way to eat the first course is by spearing the fish on a knife straight from the communal dish. The rice, too, can be eaten directly from the pan, scooping it up with a spoon and confining yourself to the portion directly in front of you – no poaching.

Clams in Tomato Sauce with Garlic

Almejas en salsa de tomate con ajo

SERVES 4

2 kg (4 lb) live bivalves, such as clams, mussels, cockles, razor shells or queen scallops

½ teaspoon saffron threads (about 12)

4 tablespoons olive oil

1 onion, finely chopped

3–4 garlic cloves, finely chopped

1 kg (2 lb) ripe tomatoes, skinned, deseeded and diced

1 tablespoon pimentón (Spanish paprika)

about 150 ml (¼ pint) red wine

salt and freshly milled black pepper

This recipe comprises a garlicky tomato sauce into which the shellfish are dropped raw. The cooking is very brief, since they only take a minute or two to open in the steam, releasing their fresh juices into the sauce.

1 Wash the shellfish in plenty of cold water, checking over and discarding any that are broken or weigh unusually heavy – they're probably dead and filled with sand. Also discard any that do not close when sharply tapped. If using mussels, scrape the shells and remove their sandy little beards. If using razor shells, remove their sandy little bag of intestine and rinse well. Leave the shellfish to spit out their sand in a bucket of cold water for a few hours – overnight is even better.

2 Toast the saffron in a dry pan for 1–2 minutes until it releases its scent – don't let it burn or it will be bitter – and drop into a cup with a little boiling water. Leave to infuse for 15 minutes or so.

3 Heat the oil in a roomy frying pan and fry the chopped onion and garlic until soft and golden – don't let them brown.

4 Add the tomatoes and allow to bubble up, mashing them until they soften. Add the pimentón, the saffron with its soaking water and the wine. Bubble up again, then turn down the heat and leave to simmer for 20 minutes or so until the sauce is thick and rich. Taste and season with salt and pepper.

5 Add the shellfish – check first to see that all are looking lively. Bubble up again, then turn down the heat, cover loosely and leave the shells to open in the steam, shaking the pan now and again to allow the top layer to drop to the bottom. Take the pan off the heat as soon as all the shells open – about 4–6 minutes, depending on size of pan and thickness of shells. Discard any shells that remain closed.

Squid Cooked in its Own Ink
Calamares en su tinta

SERVES 4

1 kg (2 lb) whole squid, including their ink

3–4 tablespoons olive oil

4–5 garlic cloves, chopped

1 teaspoon dried thyme (or a handsome fresh sprig)

1 teaspoon dried oregano (it dries naturally on the stalk; just shake it in)

2–3 bay leaves

1 small red chilli, deseeded and finely chopped

handful of celery leaves or green celery sticks, finely chopped

about 12 saffron threads

½ bottle red wine

a little sugar (optional)

salt and freshly milled black pepper

A remarkably good dish, delicate and elegant, the ink that colours and flavours the sauce has a faint taste of violets. Cuttlefish can be used instead, and some say they're even better. Fishmongers who sell the fish ready prepared will usually, if asked, provide a little bagful of ink.

1 Rinse the squid thoroughly (cephalopods are sandy creatures). If preparing your own, follow the instructions on page 94, but before discarding the innards, pick through them and rescue the silvery little ink sacks, then crush them through a sieve and reserve the liquid. If large, chop the tentacles after scraping off any 'toenails'; if small, leave them in their little bunches. Rinse your hands in cold water and they won't smell fishy.

2 Warm the oil in a roomy saucepan and add the garlic. When it begins to sizzle, add the prepared squid. Turn up the heat and stir until the flesh stiffens and turns opaque.

3 Add the herbs, chilli, celery leaves or sticks, saffron and a generous amount of pepper. Pour in the wine and bring to the boil, then turn down the heat, cover loosely and leave to simmer gently for about 40 minutes, or until the flesh is perfectly tender and the juices well reduced.

4 Stir in the reserved ink, taste and season with salt and pepper – perhaps adding a little sugar if the wine was a bit rough. Serve immediately.

Grilled Salt Cod with Red Pepper Salsa

Bacalao a la brasa con salsa romesco

SERVES 4–6

250 g (8 oz) salt cod, soaked for 48 hours in several changes of water

bitter leaves, to serve

SALSA ROMESCO

2 dried red peppers (ñoras), deseeded and soaked to swell (if you can't find these, replace with 2 tablespoons pimentón, or Spanish paprika)

2 large ripe tomatoes, cut into chunks

2 garlic cloves, crushed

1 teaspoon salt

2 tablespoons fresh breadcrumbs, fried until crisp in a little olive oil

2 tablespoons toasted almonds

1 dried red chilli, deseeded and crumbled

2 tablespoons red wine vinegar

150 ml (¼ pint) olive oil

The salty chewiness of the fish is perfectly balanced by the sweetness and richness of the salsa, a speciality of the Catalan city of Tarragona. The deep red of the sauce comes from roasting the tomatoes as well as the dried red peppers (ñoras).

1 Drain the fish and remove the bones and skin – feel carefully with your fingers. Cook fiercely under a preheated hot grill until the flesh blisters and blackens a little at the edges. Shred into small pieces.

2 Roast the peppers and tomatoes under the grill until they blister and take colour. Scrape the pulp from the skin of the peppers. Skin the tomatoes, scooping out and discarding the seeds. Drop them in a liquidizer or food processor with the garlic, salt, breadcrumbs and almonds and pulverize to a paste, or pound in a mortar with a pestle.

3 Add the crumbled red chilli and the vinegar, then add the oil gradually in a thin stream, as if making a mayonnaise, and process until the sauce is thick and shiny. Fold the shredded salt cod with the salsa and serve with bitter leaves, such as frizzy endive or chicory.

Hot-pickled Tuna

Atún en escabeche

SERVES 4

- 4 thick tuna steaks, about 1 kg (2 lb) in total
- 1 heaped tablespoon plain flour
- 1 tablespoon pimentón (Spanish paprika)
- 2 tablespoons olive oil
- 1 onion, finely sliced
- 1 garlic clove, crushed
- 1 small carrot, sliced
- 1 tablespoon chopped parsley
- 1 bay leaf, torn
- 6 peppercorns, roughly crushed
- 1 teaspoon crumbled dried oregano
- 4 tablespoons sherry vinegar (or any other good vinegar)
- salt

Tuna takes particularly well to a spice bath, a valuable method of preservation in pre-refrigeration days. For those who lived in the uplands well back from the long sea coast, it was not only useful but also added variety to the diet. Mackerel also takes happily to the treatment.

1 Sprinkle the tuna steaks with salt and leave to firm and juice for 30 minutes. Pour off any liquid, pat the fish dry and dust each steak lightly through the flour mixed with the pimentón.

2 Heat a frying pan and add half the oil. Lay the fish in the hot oil and fry for 2–3 minutes, or until the flesh is opaque and the exterior a little browned – take care not to overcook. Transfer to a shallow dish in a single layer.

3 Reheat the pan, add the remaining oil and gently fry the onion for a few minutes until soft – don't let it brown.

4 Add all the remaining ingredients and bubble up to blend the flavours and soften the carrot. Pour this warm scented bath, unstrained, over the fish. Cover with a clean cloth and leave overnight in a cool place.

5 Spoon the pickle over the fish whenever you remember. It's ready to eat in a day, better in two, best in three.

Swordfish Steaks with Garlic Sauce

Pez espada a la plancha con alioli

SERVES 4

4 swordfish steaks, about
150 g (5 oz) each

1 tablespoon olive oil

salt and freshly milled
black pepper

ALIOLI

4 large garlic cloves

1 tablespoon fresh white
breadcrumbs

juice of 1 lemon

½ teaspoon salt

300 ml (½ pint) olive oil

Swordfish and tuna are treated more like steak than fish, and are often served as the main course in a meal. The flavour is robust enough to stand up to an alioli – a garlicky mayonnaise made without eggs. For a thicker, more mayonnaise-like sauce, include a whole egg.

1 Leave the fish to soak in cold salted water for 20 minutes to firm the flesh and drain out any blood.

2 Meanwhile, make the alioli. Put the garlic cloves, breadcrumbs, lemon juice and salt in a liquidizer or food processor and process to a thick paste. Add the oil gradually in a thin stream, as if making a mayonnaise, and process until you have a thick sauce.

3 Drain the fish steaks and pat dry. Rub the cut surfaces with the oil and season with salt and pepper.

4 Heat a griddle or heavy iron frying pan until it is smoking hot. Smack on the swordfish steaks and cook them fast for 2–3 minutes each side, turning once. Serve the fish with the sauce on the side.

Sea Bream Baked with Potatoes
Besugo al horno con patatas

SERVES 4

1 sea bream, about 1.5 kg (3 lb), gutted and scaled but with the head left on

1–2 bay leaves

1 lemon, quartered

500 g (1 lb) potatoes, peeled and cut into bite-sized pieces

500 g (1 lb) onions, quartered

500 g (1 lb) firm tomatoes, cut into chunks

500 g (1 lb) green peppers, cored, deseeded and cut into chunks

about 150 ml (¼ pint) dry white wine

4 tablespoons olive oil

coarse sea salt

A simple way with a fresh fish, and one that makes an expensive luxury go further. The potatoes take the flavour of the fish, and the tomatoes and onions melt to make a rich sauce with the oil.

1 Wipe over the fish with kitchen paper and salt it lightly inside and out. Tuck the bay leaves and lemon quarters into the cavity. Cover and set aside at room temperature.

2 Arrange the vegetables in a roasting tin, pour in the wine, trickle with the oil and cover with foil, shiny-side down. Bake in a preheated oven, 180°C (350°F), Gas Mark 4, for 30 minutes or so until the potatoes are tender.

3 Remove the foil. Lay the fish on the bed of vegetables, replace the foil and bake for a further 10 minutes until the fish is cooked right through. It's ready when the thickest part feels firm to your finger.

4 Remove and leave to rest for 10 minutes to allow the heat to reach right through to the bone.

Fish Hotpot
Guiso de pescado

SERVES 4

1 kg (2 lb) white fish
  fillets

150 ml (¼ pint) olive oil

2 large onions, sliced

3–4 garlic cloves, sliced

1 tablespoon chopped
  serrano ham

1 litre (1¾ pints) fish
  stock (made with heads
  and bones, but be
  careful to remove the
  gills or the stock will
  become bitter)

300 ml (½ pint) white wine

1 bay leaf

1 kg (2 lb) yellow-fleshed
  potatoes, peeled and
  sliced lengthways

500 g (1 lb) chard or
  spinach, roughly
  shredded

salt

*Homely but classic, this is a fish stew that has no need of fancy
sauces. Ask the fishmonger for the heads and bones to make a stock.
Salt-cured cod, bacalao, can be used instead of fresh fish: soak for
48 hours in several changes of water.*

1 Skin the fish fillets if necessary and remove any
whiskery bones. Chop into bite-sized pieces. Salt lightly
and set aside.

2 Heat the oil gently in a roomy saucepan. Add the onions
and garlic, salt lightly and fry very gently for 20 minutes
or so until soft and golden – don't let them brown.

3 Add the serrano ham and the stock, wine and bay leaf
and boil rapidly until the volume has reduced by half.

4 Add the potatoes and simmer gently for 15–20 minutes
until just tender. Add the chard or spinach and bubble
up until the leaves wilt.

5 Lay in the fish, return the broth to the boil and cook
for another 4–5 minutes – just long enough for the fish to
turn opaque. Serve in deep bowls and eat with a spoon
and fork.

Vegetables & Accompaniments

Tomatoes with a Pine Nut Stuffing

Tomates rellenos con piñones

SERVES 4

4–8 ripe firm tomatoes

4 tablespoons olive oil,
plus extra for oiling

2 garlic cloves, finely
chopped

2 tablespoons pine nuts

1 tablespoon finely
chopped serrano ham
(optional)

1 tablespoon chopped
parsley

4 heaped tablespoons
fresh breadcrumbs

salt and freshly milled
black pepper

Pine nuts – the stone-pine's oily little seeds extracted with difficulty from their rock-hard shells – give a deliciously resiny flavour to this simple stuffing.

1 Wipe each tomato, then slice a little lid off the stem end and reserve. Scoop out the seeds and discard. Hollow out the tomatoes, reserving the pulp. Arrange the hollowed-out tomatoes in an oiled baking dish.

2 Warm half the oil in a small pan and fry the garlic. Add the pine nuts and let them take on a little colour. Then add the reserved tomato flesh and bubble up to make a little sauce. Stir in the ham, if using, parsley and breadcrumbs. Season with salt and pepper.

3 Stuff the tomatoes with the breadcrumb mixture. Top with the reserved lids and trickle with the remainder of the olive oil.

4 Place the tomatoes in a preheated oven, 220°C (425°F), Gas Mark 7, for 25–30 minutes. Larger tomatoes need a slightly lower temperature and a longer cooking time. Serve at room temperature.

Mixed Salad with Tuna and Egg
Ensalada mixta

SERVES 4

1 cos lettuce, thickly sliced

1 green pepper, cored, deseeded and finely sliced

2 large tomatoes, cut into chunks

2 small or ½ large cucumber, cut into chunks

½ mild Spanish onion, finely slivered

1–2 tablespoons green olives

200 g (7 oz) can tuna, drained and flaked (optional)

1–2 hard-boiled free-range eggs, shelled and quartered (optional)

6 tablespoons olive oil

2 tablespoons red or white wine vinegar or lemon juice

coarse sea salt

Salads of chunky raw vegetables and crisp cos lettuce leaves are preferred to soft-leaf salads – which are, in any event, too delicate to stand up to the heat of a Spanish summer.

1 Arrange all the salad ingredients in layers on a large flat plate, finishing with the onion rings and olives. Arrange the optional extras, if using, over the top.

2 Dress with the oil, vinegar or lemon juice and a generous pinch of coarse sea salt – don't blend into a vinaigrette first; Spain likes the taste of its olive oil. That's all.

Broad Beans with Serrano Ham
Habas con jamón

SERVES 4

1 kg (2 lb) young broad beans in their pods (or 350 g/11½ oz mature podded beans)

4 tablespoons olive oil

1 onion, diced

2–3 garlic cloves, thinly sliced

2 tablespoons diced serrano ham

about 150 ml (¼ pint) dry sherry or white wine

1 tablespoon fresh breadcrumbs

1 tablespoon chopped parsley

salt and freshly milled black pepper

Young broad beans, picked while the pods are still soft and furry, are used whole for this dish, which have a delicate flavour rather like okra and retain their fragrance during the cooking. Later in the season, discard the pods and make it with the beans alone.

1 Top, tail and string the young beans in their pods and then chop them into short lengths following the swell of each bean.

2 Warm the oil in a flameproof casserole or heavy saucepan. Fry the onion and garlic for a moment without allowing them to take any colour.

3 Add the beans, ham, sherry or wine and enough water to cover. Add salt and pepper, and bring all to the boil. Cover and stew gently for 1½ hours – this can be done on the hob or in a preheated oven, 160°C (325°F), Gas Mark 3. Check intermittently and add water if necessary.

4 When the beans are tender, allow to bubble up, uncovered, for a moment to evaporate the liquid – the beans should be juicy but not swimming. Stir in the breadcrumbs and parsley. Reheat, taste and add more salt and pepper if necessary.

Fried Green Peppers with Garlic
Pimientos fritos con ajo

SERVES 4

750 g (1½ lb) green frying peppers

about 4 tablespoons olive oil

3–4 garlic cloves, unpeeled and roughly chopped

salt

sherry vinegar, to serve (optional)

Frying peppers in Spain come in two kinds: the long, thin, torpedo-shaped dark green pods with very thin flesh and a gentle, grassy flavour; and pimientos de Padrón *which are small, triangular and equally thin-fleshed: though chilli-like in shape they are mostly mild but with a few fiery ones in every batch.*

1 Rinse the peppers and shake them dry. Don't core or deseed them but leave them whole.

2 Heat the oil in a frying pan until a faint blue haze rises. Add the peppers and fry over a high heat, turning them until all sides take a little colour. Turn the heat right down, add the garlic and salt lightly and cover the pan. Cook over a gentle heat for about 10 minutes until the peppers are soft.

3 Remove the lid and bubble up for 1–2 minutes until the oil loses its moisture and begins to clear. Allow to cool to room temperature and serve sauced with their own oily juices. Sprinkle with a few drops of sherry vinegar – or not, as you please.

Lentils with Rice
Moros y cristianos

SERVES 4

MOORS

500 g (1 lb) lentils

½ large mild onion, finely chopped

2 tablespoons olive oil

salt and freshly milled black pepper

CHRISTIANS

250 g (8 oz) white long-grain rice, boiled and drained

2 garlic cloves, chopped

1 tablespoon olive oil

TO FINISH

2 hard-boiled free-range eggs, shelled and chopped

2 tablespoons toasted almonds

This dish's name – Moors and Christians – commemorates the epic encounter at the gates of Granada when the Moors of Al-Andaluz were chased from their last stronghold by the combined might of Ferdinand of Aragón and Isabella of Castile. The combination delivers a nutritionally-perfect balance of pulses and grains.

1 For the Moors, cook the lentils in enough water to cover to a depth of 2 fingers – they'll take 40–50 minutes to soften. Season with salt and pepper and stir in the onion and oil. Bring back to the boil, allow one big bubble to let the oil form an emulsion with the lentil juices and remove from the heat and reserve.

2 Meanwhile, for the Christians, turn the rice and garlic in the oil in a roomy frying pan, then add water to cover to a depth of 2 fingers. Bubble up, turn down the heat and simmer gently for about 20 minutes until tender.

3 Pile the lentils in the middle of a hot serving dish and surround with the rice: the Moors are encircled by the Christian battalions. Finish the lentils with the chopped hard-boiled egg and the rice with the toasted almonds. Propaganda on a plate.

Artichokes with Broad Beans
Alcachofas con habas

SERVES 4–6

8–12 artichokes (depending on size)

squeeze of lemon juice or 1 teaspoon vinegar

1 large onion, finely chopped

2–3 garlic cloves, finely chopped

4 tablespoons olive oil

about 150 ml (¼ pint) white wine

250 g (8 oz) shelled broad beans (skinned, if old and leathery)

1 tablespoon chopped parsley

1 tablespoon chopped mint

1 tablespoon fresh breadcrumbs

1 tablespoon toasted flaked almonds, to garnish

salt and freshly milled black pepper

This is a classic combination from Granada's fertile market garden, the vega, known since Roman days for its succulent broad beans and fine fat artichokes. When preparing the hearts, remember that the artichoke is a member of the daisy family and that you're dealing with a flower head.

1 Prepare the artichoke hearts first: trim off the stalks close to the base. Scrape the stalks to remove the hard exterior fibres – the tender centre can be eaten – and drop into cold water with the lemon juice or vinegar. Snap off the tough outer leaves, then, with a sharp knife, cut off the tops of the remaining leaves close to the base, exposing the small leaves that protect the choke. Nick out the inner leaves and carve out the choke. Drop the prepared hearts into the water.

2 In a roomy flameproof casserole, gently fry the onion and garlic in the oil until they soften. Add the artichoke hearts and stalks. Cover and let everything fry over a low heat for 15 minutes, shaking regularly, until the artichoke begins to take a little colour.

3 Add the wine and let it all bubble up until the liquid has reduced by half. Add the shelled beans and a glass of water. Season with salt and pepper. Allow to bubble up, turn down the heat and leave to cook gently for about 15 minutes until the vegetables are tender, adding a little boiling water if necessary.

4 Stir in the chopped parsley and mint, and a handful of breadcrumbs to thicken the juices. Heap on a warm serving dish and sprinkle over the toasted almonds.

Chard with Ham and Garlic

Acelgas con jamón y ajo

Chard, also known as Swiss chard, is a robust, spinach-like vegetable with dark green leaves and pale, juicy stalks. An all-year crop, in summer it's less vulnerable to heat than spinach, and in winter it grows faster than cabbage (which, in any event, likes a touch of frost).

SERVES 4-6

1 large bunch of chard (8–12 stalks)

4 tablespoons olive oil

juice and finely grated rind of 1 lemon

4 garlic cloves, finely sliced

1 tablespoon water

1 tablespoon chopped serrano ham

1 tablespoon chopped flat leaf parsley

salt and freshly milled black pepper

1 Rinse the chard (it grows in sandy soil and may be gritty) and separate the stalks from the leaves. Shred thickly and keep the leaves and stalks separate.

2 Cook the shredded leaves in a lidded pan with a little salt and the minimum of water for about 5 minutes or so until they wilt and soften. Drain thoroughly. Toss with half the oil, and the lemon juice and rind. Season and reserve.

3 Meanwhile, rinse the stalks and slice into lengths about as fat as your finger. Heat the remaining oil in the pan and add the garlic. Add the chopped stalks and cook for a minute, then add the water and bubble up. Cover tightly and cook for about 10 minutes until perfectly tender, then stir in the ham and parsley.

4 Add pepper (no salt) and serve. You could also arrange the leaves on one side of the serving dish and the stalks on the other.

Potatoes with Almonds and Saffron
Patatas en ajopollo

SERVES 4

500 g (1 lb) potatoes, scrubbed or peeled and cut into chunks

2 tablespoons olive oil

2 tablespoons whole blanched almonds

1 garlic clove, finely chopped

1 tablespoon fresh breadcrumbs

1 tablespoon chopped parsley

12 saffron threads, soaked in 1 tablespoon boiling water

salt and freshly milled black pepper

The almond and saffron sauce, a Valencian combination, is particularly good with tender-skinned baby new potatoes. Main-crop potatoes should be peeled and cut into bite-sized chunks.

1 Drop the potatoes into salted water and set them aside.

2 Heat the oil in a small frying pan and fry the almonds until golden, then stir in the garlic and breadcrumbs. Stir over the heat until light golden brown. Add the parsley and saffron and its soaking water and allow to bubble up.

3 Tip the contents of the pan into the food processor and process with a couple of spoonfuls of water to a thick paste, or pound in a mortar with a pestle.

4 Drain the potatoes and transfer them to a heavy pan. Add the almond and saffron paste and pour in enough water to come halfway up the potatoes. Season with salt and pepper. Bring to the boil, cover and cook gently for about 15 minutes until the potatoes are nearly tender, turning them halfway through the cooking to allow the top potatoes to come into contact with the heat at the bottom.

5 Remove the lid and boil rapidly until the cooking broth is reduced to a thick sauce and the potatoes are perfectly soft. Serve at room temperature.

Braised Aubergines

Pisto de berejenas

SERVES 4

4 tablespoons olive oil

4 firm aubergines, diced

1 teaspoon cumin seeds

2 large onions, finely
sliced

salt

Gentle cooking enhances the sweetness of the onions, which contrasts with the smooth flesh and earthy flavour of the aubergines. Large, firm, meaty and purple-skinned in its Mediterranean incarnation, the aubergine cooks to a satisfying richness when paired, as here, with olive oil.

1 Heat half the oil in a heavy frying pan and gently fry the aubergines, sprinkled with the cumin seeds and a little salt, until they soften and take colour. Be patient – first they will soak up oil like a sponge and then they will release it again, which is when they begin to fry a second time. Transfer to a sieve placed over a bowl to catch the drippings.

2 Return the drippings to the pan and fry the onions until soft and lightly golden. Take your time – allow at least 20 minutes. Stir in the aubergine and cook for another 5 minutes.

3 Leave to cool to room temperature. Eat with thick slices of country bread toasted over a direct flame and rubbed with garlic, if you like; perfect with a few slivers of Manchego cheese.

Cauliflower with Garlic
Coliflor con ajo

SERVES 4

1 cauliflower

2 tablespoons olive oil, plus extra if necessary

2 garlic cloves, chopped

1 tablespoon black olives, pitted and chopped

1 teaspoon cumin seeds

1 teaspoon hot pimentón (Spanish chilli powder)

salt

This, in my experience, is just about the only way to make cauliflower taste exotic. For a touch of luxury, stir in a handful of diced serrano ham.

1 Divide the cauliflower into bite-sized florets. Cook in salted boiling water until tender, then drain.

2 Heat the oil in a roomy frying pan and fry the garlic until it softens and takes on a little colour. Add the drained cauliflower and fry for a few minutes, or until it begins to sizzle and colour slightly.

3 Add the olives, sprinkle with the cumin seeds and season with salt and the hot pimentón. Fry gently for 10 minutes or so, turning the cauliflower until it browns evenly a little all over and takes on the flavours of all the spices. Serve at room temperature.

Broad Beans with Chestnuts
Habas con castañas

SERVES 6−8

SERVES 6−8

350 g (11½ oz) dried skinned broad beans, soaked overnight in cold water

1 short length of serrano ham bone or a bacon knuckle

1 free-range chicken quarter

350 g (11½ oz) dried chestnuts, soaked overnight in cold water (or 500 g/1 lb fresh ones, skinned)

2 tablespoons olive oil

1 onion, roughly chopped

1 large carrot, chopped

1 bay leaf

1 thyme sprig

½ teaspoon crushed black peppercorns

1 short cinnamon stick

about 250 g (8 oz) pumpkin, deseeded, peeled and diced

about 2 tablespoons chopped fresh coriander

1−2 links of fresh (soft) chorizo, crumbled and fried (optional)

salt

In this dish from the sierras of Seville, dried broad beans are combined with dried chestnuts. The finishing flavouring of coriander leaves is found nowhere else in Spain, a result of trade with the pig herdsmen of Portugal, who acquired the taste from trade with the Orient.

1 Drain the beans and put them in a roomy flameproof stew pot with the ham bone or bacon knuckle and the chicken quarter. Add enough water to cover all to a depth of 2 fingers. Bring to the boil and skim off any grey foam that rises to the surface.

2 Add the drained dried (or skinned fresh) chestnuts, oil, onion, carrot, herbs and spices and bring back to the boil. Turn down the heat, cover loosely and leave to bubble gently for 1−1½ hours, or until the beans and chestnuts are perfectly soft. Add the pumpkin, return to the boil and bubble up for 15 minutes or so until the pumpkin is perfectly tender. Taste and adjust the seasoning if necessary and finish with the chopped coriander, along with crumbled fresh chorizo fried in its own oily juices, if you like.

3 Serve in deep soup plates, with red wine for the digestion and country bread for mopping.

Grilled Asparagus with Parsley Salsa
Asparagos a la parilla con salsa verde

SERVES 4

1 kg (2 lb) green
   asparagus spears
oil, for brushing
salt

SALSA

4 heaped tablespoons
   chopped flat leaf
   parsley, leaves only
2 garlic cloves, roughly
   chopped
yolk of 1 hard-boiled
   free-range egg
2 tablespoons lemon
   juice
150 ml (¼ pint) olive oil
salt

Once you've tasted grilled asparagus, you'll never want to cook them any other way. The flavour comes through clear and clean and the asparagus remains juicy and lightly blistered with caramelized juices. For grilling, you need green asparagus as thick as your thumb.

1 Wash and trim the asparagus, discarding the woody bits and peeling off any hard skin.

2 Put all the salsa ingredients except the oil into a liquidizer or food processor and process to a smooth purée. Add the oil gradually in a thin stream, as if making a mayonnaise, and process until you have a thick sauce.

3 Arrange the asparagus on a grill pan in a single layer. Brush with oil and sprinkle with salt. Cook under a preheated hot grill for about 4–5 minutes, turning to cook all sides, until they steam and blister black a little in patches. Hand round the salsa separately.

Flageolets with Chorizo
Habas verdes con longaniza y gachas de maíz

SERVES 4-6

350 g (11½ oz) green
  flageolet beans,
  soaked for 2-3 hours
  in cold water

100 g (3½ oz) serrano
  ham or lean bacon,
  diced

2-3 garlic cloves, peeled

1 bay leaf

1 small thyme sprig

½ teaspoon
  peppercorns, crushed

1 longaniza or 150 g
  (5 oz) fresh (soft)
  chorizo, sliced or
  crumbled

1 tablespoon pure pork
  lard or olive oil

250 g (8 oz) ready-
  cooked polenta

4 tablespoons chopped
  parsley

1 tablespoon chopped
  mint

salt (optional)

In northern Spain, the dried green beans the French call flageolets – dried haricots picked green – are esteemed for their delicate flavour and slightly gluey texture. In this dish from Catalonia, they're combined with the long, thin lightly smoked chorizo known as longaniza, and served with crisp cubes of polenta.

1 Drain the beans and put them with the ham or bacon in a roomy flameproof pot with the garlic, bay leaf, thyme sprig, crushed peppercorns and enough cold water to cover; beans need plenty of room to swell. Bring to the boil and skim off any grey foam that rises. Turn down the heat and simmer for about an hour until they're perfectly soft. You may need to add a little boiling water during the cooking: the beans should be juicy but not quite soupy.

2 Meanwhile, fry the longaniza or chorizo in the lard or oil until browned at the edges, then remove and set aside. Chop the polenta into dice and turn them in the pan drippings until they acquire a crisp little crust on all sides.

3 Stir the parsley and mint into the beans. Taste and add salt if necessary. Top the beans with the longaniza or chorizo and serve the crisp polenta cubes on the side.

Lentil Soup with Pork and Greens
Potage de lentejas

500 g (1 lb) pork belly

500 g (1 lb) greeny-
brown lentils

½ head of garlic (about
6 fat cloves), unpeeled

2–3 links of chorizo, or
100 g (3½ oz) shoulder
pork, diced, and
1 tablespoon pimentón
(Spanish paprika)

500 g (1 lb) canned or
fresh tomatoes,
roughly chopped

½ teaspoon cumin
seeds

2 litres (3½ pints) water

1 large potato, peeled
and cubed

250 g (8 oz) spring
greens or spinach,
shredded

2 tablespoons extra-
virgin olive oil

salt and freshly milled
black pepper

2–3 hard-boiled free-
range eggs, shelled
and quartered, to
garnish (optional)

Lentils, floury and nutty, are the fast food of the pulses, since they don't need soaking. For a soup, choose the large, greeny-brown Spanish lentils, which collapse in the pot and drink up the flavour of whatever else goes into the stew.

1 Trim the pork belly without discarding any fat – it adds flavour and the lentils will drink it all up – and then dice. Pick over the lentils, checking for any tiny stones. Spear the garlic head on a knife and hold it over a gas or candle flame until the papery skin singes and blackens a little and the flesh is lightly caramelized.

2 Put everything except the finishing ingredients into a roomy saucepan. Salt lightly and bring to the boil. Turn down the heat, cover loosely and leave to simmer gently for 40–50 minutes until the lentils are perfectly soft and beginning to collapse into the broth. Stir occasionally to avoid sticking and add a splash of boiling water if it looks like drying out.

3 When the lentils are tender, add the cubed potato. Return to the boil and turn down the heat. Cover again and cook for another 10 minutes until the potato is nearly soft – test for doneness with a knife. Stir in the spring greens or spinach and bubble for another 5 minutes. Stir in the oil and bubble up again to amalgamate it with the broth – it disappears like magic, leaving a silky smoothness without a trace of oiliness. Taste and adjust the seasoning.

4 Ladle the soup into deep bowls and finish with the hard-boiled egg quarters, if you like. Accompany with a young red wine, nothing grand – a little acidity aids the digestion.

Desserts & Cakes

Peaches in Red Wine with Cinnamon
Melocotones en vino con canela

SERVES 4

4 large, firm yellow-fleshed peaches

1 bottle strong Spanish red wine

5 cm (2 inch) cinnamon stick

2 cloves

8 peppercorns

1 bay leaf

about 4 heaped tablespoons caster sugar

juice of 1 lemon

Visually as well as gastronomically dramatic, the peaches acquire a rich burgundy velvet jacket, which, when cut open, reveals the golden flesh. Good with mantecados, *the soft, powdery almond biscuits Spanish children hope to find in their shoes on Twelfth Night, when all good Catholics receive their Christmas presents.*

1 Scald the peaches and remove their skins. Set them in a heavy saucepan that will just accommodate them.

2 Add the rest of the ingredients – the wine should just about cover the fruit. Bring to the boil, then turn down the heat to low, cover and let the pears poach very gently for about 30–40 minutes until tender. Transfer the fruit to a serving dish.

3 Bring the poaching liquid to the boil and bubble up fiercely until thick, shiny and reduced by half. Strain the syrup over the peaches.

Custard Fritters
Leche frita

SERVES 4-6

CUSTARD

6 free-range eggs

about 125 g (4 oz) plain flour

150 ml (¼ pint) milk

grated rind of ½ lemon

1 short cinnamon stick

1 teaspoon orange flower water or orange juice

125 g (4 oz) vanilla sugar

COATING

2 free-range eggs

2 tablespoons milk

about 100 g (3½ oz) finely crushed toasted breadcrumbs

oil, for deep-frying

TO DUST

ground cinnamon

caster sugar

This is Catalonia's sweet version of Andalusia's savoury croqueta. *Instead of vanilla sugar, perfume the custard with scrapings from a piece of vanilla pod or a drop of real vanilla extract, or ring the changes with cinnamon, grated orange rind or a splash of your favourite liqueur.*

1 Whisk 2 of the eggs to blend. Mix in as much of the flour as the liquid will accept to make a stiff paste. Whisk another 4 eggs separately, then beat them into the paste, working until smooth.

2 Bring the milk to the boil in a heavy saucepan with the lemon rind and cinnamon stick. Remove from the heat and leave to cool.

3 Whisk in the egg mixture, beating until smooth, and bring gently towards the boil, stirring continuously. Just before it boils, cool it down with the orange flower water or orange juice. Stir in the vanilla sugar. Continue to cook gently, but without allowing it to boil, until thick enough to set when you drop a blob on a cold saucer.

4 Line a baking tray with clingfilm and pour in a layer of the custard as thick as your thumb. Leave to cool, cover with another sheet of clingfilm and transfer to the refrigerator to firm for a few hours, or overnight if possible.

5 Cut the custard into bite-sized fingers, squares or triangles for coating. Beat the remaining 2 eggs on one plate with the milk and spread the breadcrumbs on another plate. Pass the custard shapes first through the egg and milk mixture to coat thoroughly, then press gently into the breadcrumbs, making sure all sides are covered. Check that there are no gaps – if so, repair them with a dab of

egg and a sprinkle of crumbs. Set them back in the refrigerator for another hour or so to set the jackets – or freeze until you're ready to cook.

6 Heat a saucepan of oil for deep-frying until a faint blue haze rises. Slip in the custard fritters straight from the refrigerator, a few at a time so that the oil temperature remains high, and fry, turning them once, until crisp and brown.

7 Remove carefully with a draining spoon and transfer to kitchen paper to drain. Dust with cinnamon and sugar, and serve piping hot, before they lose their crispness. Delicious with a salad of sliced oranges dressed with honey, or fresh strawberries in season.

Chocolate and Cinnamon Ice Cream

Helado de chocolate con canela

SERVES 4

50 g (2 oz) best-quality dark chocolate (at least 70% cocoa solids)

150 ml (¼ pint) plus 450 ml (¾ pint) hot (not boiling) water

1 teaspoon ground cinnamon

2 free-range egg yolks

4 tablespoons condensed milk or double cream plus 4 tablespoons caster sugar

The ladies of the Spanish court were the first to taste the addictive joys of drinking chocolate, unknown in the Old World before Columbus made landfall in the New. In Spain, where it's a pick-me-up after a night on the tiles, it's usually spiced with cinnamon.

1 Break the chocolate into small pieces and soften it very gently over a low heat in a small saucepan with the 150 ml (¼ pint) hot water. As soon as it liquefies, whisk in the larger quantity of hot water. Add the cinnamon and whisk until perfectly smooth. Remove from the heat.

2 Beat the egg yolks with the condensed milk or cream and sugar and whisk the mixture into the hot liquid. Stir it over a gentle heat until the mixture thickens enough to coat the back of a wooden spoon.

3 Freeze in an ice cream maker according to the manufacturer's instructions. Alternatively, put in a lidded freezerproof container in the freezer until almost solid. Tip it into a liquidizer or food processor and process briefly to break up the ice crystals, then freeze again until firm.

4 Remove from the freezer about 20 minutes or so before you're ready to serve to allow it to soften. If you like, finish each portion with a trickle of Pedro Ximenes, the thick, black maple-syrupy sherry made from the grapes of the same name, and a sprinkle of toasted almonds.

Orange Caramel Custard
Flan de naranja

SERVES 4-6

CARAMEL

4 tablespoons caster sugar

2–3 tablespoons water

CUSTARD

450 ml (¾ pint) freshly-squeezed orange juice

3 whole free-range eggs, plus 3 yolks

2–3 tablespoons caster sugar

The everyday version of a popular dessert loved by all Spanish children, found on every restaurant menu from Bilbao to Cádiz. It is usually made with milk and a packet mix but in this sophisticated Valencian version, it is made with freshly-squeezed orange juice – packet orange juice won't do. If you prefer a dairy version, simply replace the juice with full-cream milk.

1 Make the caramel in a small saucepan. Melt the dry sugar, stirring all the time with a wooden spoon, over a steady heat until the sugar caramelizes a rich chestnut brown. This will take only a moment or two.

2 Add the water off the heat – be careful, as it will splutter. Stir over a low heat until you have thick, dark syrup. Divide this caramel into 4–6 individual cocottes or mini soufflé dishes if that's your preference. Tip to coat the base.

3 Heat the oven to 150°C (300°F), Gas Mark 2. For the custard, beat together the orange juice, whole eggs, egg yolks and sugar until well blended. Divide the mixture among the cocottes or mini soufflé dishes.

4 Transfer the cocottes to a roasting tin and pour in enough boiling water to come halfway up the cocottes. Cover the whole thing in foil and transfer to the preheated oven. Cook for 25–30 minutes or until the custard is just set. The set is delicate but it will firm a little more as it cools.

5 Serve at room temperature in their cooking dishes, with a crisp biscuit to dip in the caramel sauce which forms beneath the custard.

Spiced Almond Shortbreads
Mantecados

MAKES ABOUT 24

500 g (1 lb) pure pork lard, plus extra for greasing

500 g (1 lb) caster sugar

4 free-range egg yolks

finely grated rind and juice of 1 lemon

1 kg (2 lb) plain flour

500 g (1 lb) ground almonds

1 tablespoon ground cinnamon

These melt-in-the-mouth Christmas cookies – also known as polverones (dusty biscuits) – are a treat for good children when the Three Wise Men come to visit the Christ child on 6 January. The rich, powdery shortbread is shortened with lard rather than butter.

1 In a large bowl, beat the lard until it softens, then beat in the sugar and whisk until fluffy. Beat in the egg yolks and lemon rind.

2 Sift in the flour and beat it a little more. Then fold in the ground almonds and cinnamon. Add a tablespoonful of lemon juice and work it some more until you have a soft dough.

3 Roll out the dough to the thickness of the width of your thumb and cut out rounds with a small wine glass.

4 Transfer the cookies to a lightly greased baking tray. Place in a preheated oven, 190°C (375°F), Gas Mark 5, for 20 minutes, and then reduce the oven to 180°C (350°F), Gas Mark 4, and bake for another 15–20 minutes, or until the cookies are pale gold.

5 Transfer the cookies carefully to a wire rack to cool – they're very crumbly. Wrap each cookie in a scrap of tissue paper and store in an airtight tin.

St James's Almond Tart

Pastel de santiago

SERVES 6−8

PASTRY

100 g (3½ oz) pure pork
  lard or unsalted butter

100 g (3½ oz) caster
  sugar

1 free-range egg

1 teaspoon ground
  cinnamon

about 200 g (7 oz) plain
  flour, plus extra for
  dusting

FILLING

8 free-range eggs

500 g (1 lb) caster sugar

500 g (1 lb) ground
  almonds

juice and finely grated
  rind of 1 lemon

icing sugar, for dusting

This rich, lemony tart was baked to fortify pilgrims on the long walk to Santiago de Compostela, the shrine of St James. The lemon is for the sorrow of Good Friday and the almonds, grown from stock from the Jordan Valley, serve as a reminder of the Holy Land.

1 Make the pastry first. Beat the lard or butter with the sugar until light and fluffy. Beat in the egg and cinnamon. Using your hand or a food processor, work in enough flour to make a smooth, softish paste. Work the paste into a ball, cover with clingfilm and leave to firm for 30 minutes. Roll it out very thinly on a floured surface and use to line a tart tin 22 cm (8½ inches) in diameter and no less than 5 cm (2 inches) deep. Save any pastry scraps to bake as biscuits.

2 Now make the filling. Whisk the eggs until light and fluffy, then sprinkle in the sugar spoonful by spoonful and continue to beat until white and doubled in volume. Keep going – even with machinery the process takes longer than you think. Gently fold in the ground almonds and lemon juice and rind. Spoon the mixture into the tart base – it can come right up to the edge because it shrinks as it sets. Don't overfill: if you have any left over, bake it in little madeleine tins or as cupcakes.

3 Place in a preheated oven, 200°C (400°F), Gas Mark 6, for 45–50 minutes, or until the pastry is crisp and the topping firm and beautifully browned.

4 Unmould. When cool, finish with a dusting of icing sugar with a scallop shell on the surface. You can, if you wish, spread a layer of Quince Paste (see page 155) or damson jam on the tart base before you top it with the almond mixture – if so, give the pastry base 10 minutes in a hot oven first, just long enough to set the surface.

Yeast Cakes with Almonds and Fruit
Cocas con almendras y frutas confitadas

SERVES 6-8

1 kg (2 lb) strong bread flour, plus extra for dusting

½ teaspoon salt

1 tablespoon easy-blend dried yeast

1 teaspoon finely grated lemon rind

4 free-range eggs

100 ml (3½ fl oz) mild olive oil, plus extra for oiling

250 g (8 oz) caster sugar

about 500 ml (17 fl oz) warm milk

MARZIPAN

150 g (5 oz) ground almonds

150 g (5 oz) caster sugar

1 free-range egg yolk

TO FINISH

1 free-range egg, beaten with 1 tablespoon water

2 tablespoons chopped crystallized fruit

Purists will tell you that the true coca, *as prepared in the Levant and on the Balearic islands, is a primitive flat bread. Pay no attention; this festive version topped with marzipan and crystallized fruit is much more delicious.*

1 Sift the flour with the salt into a warm bowl. Mix in the yeast and lemon rind. Make a well in the flour mixture and add the eggs, oil and sugar. Work in enough warm milk to make a soft dough. Knead well until the dough forms a ball that leaves the side of the bowl clean. Cover with clingfilm – stretch it over the top so that it makes a little warm hothouse with plenty of room for the dough to expand – and leave in a warm place until doubled in size. It will take at least 2 hours: this is a very rich dough that takes longer to rise than a plain dough.

2 Meanwhile, make the marzipan. Work the ground almonds and sugar with the egg yolk until you have a soft, spreadable paste – you may need a little water.

3 When the dough has doubled in size, knock it back and knead it vigorously to distribute the air bubbles, then form the dough into a ball. Cut the ball into 6–8 equal-sized pieces, knead again and pat or roll out each piece into a rectangle no thicker than the width of your thumb. Transfer the rectangles to an oiled and flour-dusted baking sheet. Spread each piece with the marzipan, leaving a narrow margin around the edges.

4 To finish, prick the breads in a few places with a fork, brush with the egg and water mixture and sprinkle with the crystallized fruit. Cover with clingfilm and leave to rise again for another 20–30 minutes.

5 Place the breads in a preheated oven, 180°C (350°F), Gas Mark 4, for 30–40 minutes until well risen and light. The marzipan will toast and firm – if it looks like burning before the dough has risen, cover with foil. Transfer to a wire rack to cool. Perfect served with a chilled glass of agua de Valencia – cava on ice with orange juice.

Madeira Cake with Olive Oil
Biscocho de aceite

SERVES 6−8

200 g (7 oz) plain flour

50 g (2 oz) ground almonds

2 level teaspoons baking powder

250 ml (8 fl oz) light olive oil (not extra-virgin), plus extra for oiling

4 free-range eggs, lightly whisked

250 g (5 oz) caster sugar

juice and finely grated rind of 1 small Seville orange or lemon

This is a basic four-quarter cake made with olive oil rather than butter; anyone with a nut allergy can replace the ground almonds with the same weight of flour. Pick a mild rectified olive oil rather than extra-virgin – but if virgin is all you have, bring it up to frying-temperature and then allow to cool before using.

1 Mix the dry ingredients together first, then tip everything into a food processor and beat until the mixture is smooth and free of lumps. Easy, isn't it?

2 Oil a 1 kg (2 lb) loaf tin and line the base with greaseproof paper. Drop in the cake mixture (soft dropping consistency is what you're looking for), and spread it into the corners.

3 Place in a preheated oven, 180°C (350°F), Gas Mark 4, for 45–50 minutes until the cake is well risen, firm to the finger and has shrunk from the sides. Wait until it cools a little before you tip it out and transfer it to a wire rack to cool completely. If you store it in an airtight tin it will keep for at least a month.

Nut Milk Granita

Granita de horchata

MAKES ABOUT
1.5 LITRES
(2½ PINTS)

**250 g (8 oz) whole
blanched almonds**

**about 2 tablespoons
caster sugar (more
if you like)**

1 short cinnamon stick

Horchata, a legacy of the Moorish presence in Andalusia, is an infusion of crushed nuts and water flavoured with cinnamon and lightly sweetened with sugar. As a thirst-quencher, it's served in a long glass, well iced, and is sold in refreshment bars in southern Spain throughout the summer.

1 Put the almonds into a liquidizer with about 300 ml (½ pint) water and process to a thick cream. Add enough water to make the volume up to 1 litre (1¾ pints) and leave to infuse overnight.

2 Next day, strain the milky liquid into a saucepan, stir in the sugar and add the cinnamon stick. Bring to the boil and then leave to cool. Remove the cinnamon stick.

3 Freeze in an ice cream maker according to the manufacturer's instructions. Alternatively, put in a lidded freezerproof container in the freezer until almost solid. Tip it into the liquidizer or a food processor and process to break up the ice crystals, then freeze again until firm.

4 Remove from the freezer about 10 minutes before you need it, and crush the mixture again before you serve it.

Quince Paste
Dulce de membrillo

MAKES ABOUT
1 KG (2 LB)

2 kg (4 lb) ripe quinces

1.5 litres (2½ pints)
water

about 1 kg (2 lb)
preserving sugar

oil, for oiling

Quinces ripen and soften in store, and are ready when you can smell their perfume. This fine preserve is a traditional Christmas treat, usually eaten with a slice of mature Manchego cheese.

1 Wipe and roughly chop the quinces – don't core or peel them – then put them in a preserving pan with the water.

2 Bring to the boil, then turn down to a steady simmer and cook until the quince flesh is soft – don't boil them too long or they will turn red and the colour of the paste will be too dark.

3 Push the flesh, juice and all, through a sieve. Weigh the pulp and stir in 500 g (1 lb) sugar for each 500 g (1 lb) fruit.

4 Put into a saucepan and bring very gently back to the boil, stirring until all the sugar has completely dissolved. Spread the paste in a very lightly oiled baking tray and leave in a preheated oven, 110°C (225°F), Gas Mark ¼, to dry out overnight. Alternatively, simmer, stirring throughout, for about 30–35 minutes until the pulp pulls away from the side of the pan and then spread it in the baking tray to set.

5 When cool, cut the paste into squares, wrap in greaseproof paper and store in a tin in a dry cupboard. It darkens and firms as it matures.

Index

Acknowledgements

Executive Editor: Eleanor Maxfield
Senior Editor: Sybella Stephens
Art Direction and Design: Tracy Killick
Design Concept: Smith & Gilmour
Photographer: Noel Murphy
Home Economist: Sue Henderson
Home Economist's Assistants: Rachel Wood and Paul Jackman
Stylist: Wei Tang
Production: Caroline Alberti